One Woman, One Voice

Plays by

Sharon Morgan

Christine Watkins

Lucy Gough

Lucinda Coxon

Gwenno Dafydd

Edited by

Hazel Walford Davies

PARTHIAN BOOKS

Parthian Books
53 Colum Road
Cardiff
CF10 3EF
www.parthianbooks.co.uk

First published in 2000.
All rights reserved.
© Parthian Books
ISBN 1-902638-08-5

Typeset in Galliard by NW.
Printed and bound by ColourBooks, Dublin.
With support from the Parthian Collective.

The publishers would like to thank the Arts Council of
Wales for support in the publication of this book.

Cover: Lost for Words by Sarah Snazell, from a private
collection - thanks to Mr C Burman

'When Father Papered the Parlour': words and music
by R P Weston and Fred Barnes, copyright 1909,
Francis Day and Hunter Ltd, London WC2H 0QY.

A CIP catalogue record for this book is available from
the British Library.

Contents

Modulations of Monologue

'The medium of drama is not words, but persons moving about on a stage using words'. As so often, Ezra Pound's own words don't make complete sense. But they do make common sense. We certainly don't normally describe as drama words that are divorced from physical movement, action, entrances and exits, or (Noël Coward's nightmare) bangings into the furniture. But, in turn, these perambulations are themselves as nothing without language. Mime, for example, is a great and entertaining art, but you can't do *King Lear* in it; or, if you can, it is only because the words of *King Lear* are, however voicelessly, being appealed to. Words may not be, as W.B. Yeats once put it, the only 'certain good', but we cannot begin even to think, let alone imagine, without them. They are at the heart of what it feels like to be human. They remain the basic currency, and nothing emphasises more their power of purchase than that particular dramatic form, the Monologue, where words have *plenary* power, where they are not pressed simply into literal action.

Even then, the term 'monologue' is jostled from all sides by all sorts of other, cognate forms. How, for example, does a monologue worth our attention differ from, say, mere thought ('Sometimes I just sits and thinks. . .'), from workaday speech (any natural, memorable outburst you can think of), from a crucial political 'speech' ('I have a dream today. . . '), from a lyric poem ('When I consider how my light is spent. . . '), from a song ('O the lark in the clear air . . .') or - back within the fold of drama proper - a soliloquy ('To be or not to be . . .')? Of course, on a small enough sample, there need be no difference at all. Indeed, one of the great achievements of the monologue form is that it breaks down barriers of form. It is not so much hedged about as edged around by them. There is no reason why a monologue cannot even contain, or modulate in and out of, say, song, poetry, or a tangential, extended 'aside', even within what is already a basically soliloquizing mode. The soliloquy proper, of course, has more the air of what Frank Kermode recently called 'speech in silence, the speech of silence'. Even though it might momentarily address an audience, a soliloquy normally acts as if there were no audience there to address, as if the words are not, in a sense, spoken at all. Whether across footlights or over the airwaves, a monologue has a more solid sense of an audience addressed, overheard, or listened to. Christopher Ricks once described the unusual genre of the Masque as 'different from either a poem or a play, while still making use of what plays and poems do'. The same can be said of the monologue.

The monologue forgoes the need for Pound's 'persons moving about on a stage', and yet still has to activate, in the viewer/listener's imagination, persons, movements, places. It can by all means use descriptive language, but it cannot afford to be mere description, like an essay, any more than it can afford to be all narrative, like a short story. It cannot, either, be merely the undistilled outpouring of the writer's own joys, despairs or dreams. Those emotions have to be 'personative' and 'impersonative' - terms used by the novelist Thomas Hardy even of his poems - creating, that is to say, a speaker that is never just the writer herself or himself.

However, the best analogy for the theatrical or broadcast monologue, of the kind represented in this volume, is still an analogy with poetry. But a particular *form* of poetry: the 'dramatic monologue' - as in Robert Browning's 'My Last Duchess', T.S. Eliot's 'Portrait of a Lady' or Pound's own 'Portrait d'une Femme'. This is not to expect from a monologue the rhythmic form or the consistent metaphoric life that makes a poem, though rhythmic form and metaphors will certainly play their part. It is, rather, to expect that one woman or one man's voice should be *this* woman's or *this* man's voice. The voice must reveal a vivid invented character, and all through the medium of words. At the same time, as with a 'dramatic monologue' in poetry, a theatrical or broadcast monologue must have the power to evoke also the vividness of a situation or a predicament - again out of pure language. Whatever it needs - persons, things, movements - these have to be achieved without their literal appearance on stage (the occasional glass of water or sound- or lighting-effects notwithstanding). A monologue of this kind may not need the precision-focus of a Browning 'dramatic monologue' -

> Nay, we'll go
> Together down, sir! Notice Neptune, tho'
> Taming a sea-horse, thought a rarity

Which Claus of Innsbruck cast in bronze for me

- where those 24 words evoke speaker, listener, movement, object and response all at once. But the theatrical or broadcast monologue still has its work cut out to remind us that, *pace* Ezra Pound, the medium of drama, ultimately, *is* words. And the monologue has also to remind itself that, having volunteered to forgo a cast, scenery, scene-changes, the very different soundboard of dialogue, or the accidentally-overheard, fly-on-the-wall power of soliloquy, a monologue must use its words all the more capaciously. Traditionally, actors are described as 'treading the boards'. To borrow a phrase from a poem by Philip Larkin, monologues are a case of words, just words, 'inventing where they tread'.

*   *   *   *

The five dramatists and seven monologues collected here have been chosen because they display these aspects, not as artificial requirements, but as organic qualities, in degrees varying according to the individual vision that drives each work. Each is in its own way what Lucy Gough calls a 'landscape of imagination'. Each knows, in Sharon Morgan's words, that 'she could be another woman/ But she wants to be herself'. Each knows, in Lucinda Coxon's words, of 'the other little girl, who wasn't me but could have been'. And each knows (irony being one of the moods most deliciously made room for by monologue) that 'of course she could have died here, if she'd made the effort'. That all these quoted claims come from the monologues themselves shows how alertly circumspect the form itself can afford to be. 'It is hard these days,' says the already ambiguous speaker in Lucinda Coxon's piece, 'to be ourselves'. But what is powerful is the wide range of human emotion and experience, of pleasure and of tragedy, that this negotiability of identity allows, quietly, to emerge.

Sharon Morgan's *Magic Threads* is woven around both a literal and a metaphoric 'quilt' of memory. The bed-quilt is not just parti-coloured; made from actual pieces of family clothing, it evokes a family's history, inseparable from the collective unconscious of a race. Its magic realism evinces not only the question 'Who am I?' but also 'What is a Welsh woman?'

Christine Watkins's *Welcome to My World* features the tortured questionings of Ada, a Builth Wells spinster who has recently buried her crazed mother. It is addressed to her sister who vanished mysteriously at the age of four and has now, equally mysteriously, reappeared. A deft mixing of the comic and the tragic powerfully evokes, not only fear and madness, but also submerged and suppressed memories. Christine Watkins's *Queen of Hearts* is equally witty and disturbing. The 82 year old Annie imagines the bizarre appearance of the dead Diana, Princess of Wales, in an Aberbargoed park. The monologue explores the fears and fantasies of Annie's flatmate, Raye, a young highly-disturbed transvestite besotted with

Diana, and Annie's own robust take on the strange obsessive world she is locked into.

During the course of Lucy Gough's *The Red Room*, Charlotte Brontë travels into an imaginary landscape of ice and snow. Strongly theatrical in a stage sense (the apostles cupboard, the sound effects), it still shows a mind engaged with what words on their own can best present - the *feel* of things and people not actually on stage. In Lucy Gough's *The Tail*, an anorexic girl, on the edge of womanhood, is reacting to how her body is changing. She is also, in her bath, on the edge of the flow of consciousness and shapeshiftings evoked by water. Freed in this way, the piece becomes the monologue of a mermaid.

Lucinda Coxon's *I am Angela Brazil* 'is a piece for a woman in her mid-forties' but 'to be played by a male actor'. This prefatory direction then feeds immediately into an opening flourish by the actual actor: 'I am not, of course, Angela Brazil' ('I am not prince Hamlet, nor was meant to be . . .'), so the illusion of theatre is both broken and confirmed at the very outset, thereby objectifying the shame unfolded in the various aspects of the life of this particular Angela Brazil of the text.

Gwenno Dafydd's *No Regrets* came into monologue form indirectly, and yet, on a different view, from a very direct, significant source - that of song. The author, having lived in Belgium in the early 1980s, being fluent in French and blest with an expressive singing voice, performed frequently back in Wales in French cabaret. Edith Piaf's songs are, of course, a crucial part of that musical form, and the author accepted an invitation to link the sung texts within a one-speaker context. The result enables the author to contract and distil earlier episodes in the speaker's life and merge them with the speaker's here-and-now. It makes moving room for the direct speech of a former, as well as a present, self. 'Moving room' - there's a metaphor to ponder.

Perhaps nothing highlights the nature of monologue as a form better than this otherwise odd connection with song. The idiom of monologue is, of course, spoken words, not song, but song is still a good name for the resonances that can be contained within spoken words. Song suggests the sap and sheer expressiveness of all spontaneous (or craftedly spontaneous) forms, including the expressed and implied monologues of others, their madnesses and their loves. It is no wonder, therefore, that so many of the monologues collected here use song itself as an ingredient. 'Are You Lonesome Tonight', beautifully, sadly sung by Jim Reeves or '*Dwedwch fawrion o wybodaeth / O ba beth y gwnaethpwyd hiraeth*', beautifully, sadly sung by a whole culture, convince us even half-way through just listening to them. The work of words displayed in these monologues shows that this power comes even when the words are not, as Ezra Pound called them, those of 'persons moving about on a stage'.

Hazel Walford Davies
The University of Wales, Aberystwyth

SHARON MORGAN

Sharon Morgan was born in Carmarthenshire and educated at Llandyfaelog Primary School and Queen Elizabeth's Grammar School for Girls, Carmarthen. She then proceeded to the University of Wales, Cardiff, where she graduated with a degree in History. She began her career as an actress in 1970 with Theatr Cymru, and since then she has worked extensively in theatre, film, television and radio. In 1998 she won a BAFTA award for her performance as Mary Murphy in *Tair Chwaer (Three Sisters)*, a Gaucho production for S4C.

She has translated and adapted Simone de Beauvoir's *Monologue* for the stage and played the role of Muriel in Theatr y Byd's tour of *Desperate Hopes and Fragile Dreams*. The first version of *Magic Threads* was read at the 1996 National Eisteddfod at Llandeilo in Welsh, entitled *Ede Hud*. Sharon Morgan has written for Radio Cymru's *Ponty* and for S4C's *Y Palmant Aur*. She is currently writing an urban thriller.

Ede Hud was premièred in Welsh at St Peter's Hall, Carmarthen, 25 November 1997. It was subsequently performed at Chapter Arts Centre, 26 and 27 November 1997; Brynaman Hall, 28 November 1997; and Clwb y Bont, Pontypridd, 29 November 1997.

Woman	Sharon Morgan
Designer	Penni Bastic
Lighting	Ceri James
Director	Catrin Edwards

Magic Threads

by Sharon Morgan

*Off-stage we hear a woman singing 'Hiraeth' as the
lights go up slowly on stage.*

"Dwedwch fawrion o wybodaeth
O ba beth y gwnaethpwyd hiraeth,
A pa ddefnydd a rhoid ynddo
Na ddarfyddai wrth ei wishgo.

Derfydd aur a derfydd arian
Derfydd melfed, derfydd shidan.
Derfydd pob dilledyn helaeth
Ond er hyn ni dderfydd hiraeth.

Hiraeth mawr a hiraeth creulon
Hiraeth sydd yn torri 'nghalon.
Pan fwyf dryma'r nos yn cysgu
Fe ddaw hiraeth ac am deffry.

The woman enters.

Hiraeth, hiraeth, cilia, cilia,
Paid â phwyso mor drwm arna'i.
Nesa dipyn at yr erchwyn
Gad i mi gael cysgu gronyn."

A woman on a mountain mumbling,
A woman on a mountain mumbling old songs.

She is not invisible.
Everyone can see her
From a distance
Like Paxton's Tower.
A woman on a mountain mumbling old songs.

Once upon a time there was a little girl sitting in her
grandmother's garden, she wore a frilly pink dress, a scrunchy
lacy, frilly pink dress, with beautiful pearl buttons and a big
bow at the back. Her grandmother's garden was full of flowers -
dahlias, orange and spiky, purple pom-poms and papery red
poppies, china pink roses and yellow Easter daisies, blue
aubretia and white snow on the mountain and rhubarb and
plum trees and apple trees and strawberries and raspberries and
gooseberries and blackberries and blackcurrants and red
currants, and her grandmother made rhubarb tart and raspberry
tart and blackberry tart and redcurrant and blackcurrant and
apple tart and pear tart and plum tart and jam and chutney and

Welsh cakes, and her grandmother worked in the tin works and her grandmother made ginger beer.

There she is, there she is, I can see her, with her white hair and her big apron going down the green roads with the sun like butter in the lazy afternoons when time was on stop in the faraway summers. She's wandered from her garden, her fruity flowery civilised garden, she's searching in the hedges for wild forbidden plants. With her apron full, she goes back to the secrets of her kitchen. In the darkness of her pantry, in the depth of her saucepan she creates DYNAMITE.

Taste the mountain
Taste the stream
Swallow the earth
And swallow the dream.
Suck the seed
And suck the power
Drink the rain
And eat the flower.
Smell of the sun at the end of the day
Smell of the peat
And smell of the hay.
Magic drink,
Enchanting drink,
It's the world's most powerful drink.
A small little drop and I'm not here,

A small little drop and I'm nowhere near.
I'm going up and up and up,
Higher and higher and higher,
Far above the valley,
Far above Pentyrcan and Mynydd Llysu,
I'm swallowing blue sky
I'm playing in the stars.

Song - "Mi Glywaf Dyner Lais"

"Mi glywaf dyner lais
Yn galw arnaf fi
I ddod i olchi meiau'i gyd
Yn..."
        Mixes into -

Song - "I'm Forever Blowing Bubbles"

"I'm forever blowing bubbles
Pretty bubbles in the air
They fly so high they nearly reach the sky
And then they burst and fade and..."

Stop it, stop it, Aunty Maggie doesn't like comic songs.

Once upon a time there was a little girl in a shiny flowery dress, blue and pink and puce and smudgy orange and green, stamping her foot in the mind your own business and swinging on the swing watching her grandmother crocheting gloves and dresses and sugar hats and making rag mats all the colours of the rainbow, rag mats to kneel upon, rag mats to pray upon.

Now I lay me down to sleep
Pray the Lord my soul to keep
If I die before I wake
Pray the Lord my soul to take.

And the little girl slept in a featherbed underneath the quilt her mother's mother's mother made out of her aunty's dresses and her uncles' trousers, and the little girl slept in the dreams of her relations.

Song - "Huna Blentyn"

"Huna Blentyn ar fy mynwes
Clyd a chynnes ydyw hon
Breichiau mam sy'n dynn amdanat
Cariad mam sy' dan fy mron.
Ni chaiff ddim amharu'th gyntun
Ni wna undyn â thi gam.
Huna'n dawel f'annwyl blentyn
Huna'n fwyn ar fron dy fam."

Watch yourself! It's small but it's sharp just like me. Don't come too close you could get hurt! She's sewing her children's lives so she doesn't forget. A summer afternoon over there, a winter's morning over here, a night in October, a night in the spring, the clothes that sat down with them, that felt with them, the warmth of their bodies, their hearts beating, the sweat on their backs, shivers down the spine, a skirt running, a dress lying on the grass smelling the heather, a suit praying, a blouse gardening, standing in the graveyard, crying in the bedroom. Sewing minutes, sewing hours together, best clothes and everyday clothes, sewing them together, sewing them tightly, holding them tight, feeling them in my arms. Don't come too close.

Wil bach's coat when he fell from the cart
Annie's wedding dress,
Jack's working trousers,
Jo's Madeira coat,
Jennie's dress when she won the Llangadog Eisteddfod.
Rhys's best shirt
Dai's flannel shirt
Maggie's blouse to come back from hospital,
Hetty's skirt when she was in service in Ammanford
Dora's everyday dress
Mary's America dress
Ceri's school blazer.

Watch yourselves, or you'll get hurt! It's me that remembers, it's me that wants to, the children won't remember. A quilt like a shawl my girl, no-one can come near you. I keep you safe all night with my needle, it's sharp and it's prickly like me. I choose the pieces, pieces of life, hope and fear, and shame and loss and celebration. Don't come too close, it could be dangerous.

And the little girl knew every square of material and she slept safely all night long and above the bed hung a little plaster angel with her head on one side.

Song - "Si Hei Lwli"

"Si hei lwli mabi
Mae'r llong yn mynd i ffwrdd.
Si fy mabi lwli.
Mae'r capten ar y bwrdd
Si hei lwli lws.
Cysga cysga mabi tlws
Si hei lwli mabi
Mae'r llong yn mynd i ffwrdd."

And the little girl visited the dead and the dying, taking flowers from her grandmother's garden in a cloud of gyp like magical snow, and her grandmother went to chapel three times on a Sunday in a black suit with tiny pink roses and a big shiny black hat with one big pink rose.

The woman sings the phrase.

"Rhosyn Saron yw fy enw"

That mixes into -

"Rwy'n wyn fel y lili fach dyner
Sy'n gwynu yng ngwawl Calfari"

Annie was saved and baptised in the Llwchwr
On the side of the mountain,
Aunty Hetty her sister
Kept a space for the Saviour
Everyday at her table,
A knife and fork for Jesus Christ
Breakfast supper and tea.
She loved the narrowness,
Delighted in the dogma,
Condemning lipstick, sideburns and Catholics.
No whistling on a Sunday, no knitting, no bouncing the ball, no
peeling potatoes, only making rice pudding and sitting in
uncomfortable clothes and a hat on elastic and stockings called
American tan.
Her grandmother found the power euphoric.
Everything was so clear,
So strong, as exciting

As riding down the valley
On her bike
With her feet on the handlebars
With the wind in her wild auburn hair,
Or sliding down the side of the tip
On an old piece of zinc
Laughing at mortality.
So exciting, so clear,
She was so strong, she felt no fear.
Definite, determined,
One foot on the hearth
Whistling as she turns the Welsh cakes on the plank.
Omniscient,
Omnipotent,
And in a picnic on top of the mountain
In the middle of the reeds and the heather and the sheep she sang
She sang Happy Day.

The woman sings.

"Happy Day Happy Day when Jesus washed my sins away"

Her power was pagan
It came out of the mountain earth
Mountain water ran in her veins
She worshipped what she wanted

She had no schooling
She WAS GOD and she loved her to bits.

Song - *"Rwy'n Fy Ngharu Rwyf yn Gwybod*
Mai fy eiddo byth wyf fi.
Rwy'n fy ngharu DIOLCH I FI."

Once upon a time there was a little girl sitting in her great
grandmother's garden, her mother's mother's mother who made
the quilt that kept her safe all night, who married at 18, who
had an 18-inch waist and who had 18 children. She was sitting
under the cherry tree at the bottom of the garden, cleaning
shoes, cleaning <u>14</u> pairs of shoes, shining 'til she saw her face,
and the little girl's mother's mother's father's mother bled to
death at the side of the road on her way to work in the candle
factory.

Song - *"Beth yw'r Haf i mi"*

"Beth yw'r haf i mi
Dim ond gaeaf llwm a dagrau'n lli
Er pan gollaist di
Nid yw hirddydd haf yn ddim i mi."

They were going for a walk to Auntie Mari's house again
Auntie Mari's old shell of a house on the side of the mountain
Auntie Mari who smoked a clay pipe

And never wore knickers
And peed standing up
And had a one-eyed dog called Nel.
And her mother happened to mention
That Aunty Mari's mother
Had died by the side of the road.
Her mother didn't know her name
Her mother's mother's father's mother,
A woman with no name
And four children
Dying on the side of the road.
Bleeding to death.

Was it early in the morning?
Ws there dew still on the grass?
What was she wearing
Young, nameless woman
When she went to work to die
Before reaching thirty?

It happened all of a sudden,
All of a sudden
The life flooded out
Like a red river.
Wasn't there anyone about?
Wasn't anyone awake?
Was it on a summer's morning?

Was there dew still on the grass?
It happened all of a sudden.
She must have been screaming
Was the sun shining?
Was she afraid?
She had to stop in the end
For the red river to flow.
She had to kneel,
She had to fall,
She had to lie down on the grass,
And leave the morning
And leave the summer
And leave the world
Like the little soul inside.
She feels a dewdrop on her face
She feels a teardrop on her cheek
She thinks about her children cwtshing fast asleep.
Her mother's mother's father's mother
Bleeding to death by the side of the road.
I hope the weather was nice.

Song - "Beth yw'r Haf i mi"

"Beth yw'r haf i mi
Dim ond gaeaf llwm a dagrau'n lli
Er pan gollaist di
Nid yw hirddydd haf yn ddim i mi."

Once upon a time there was a little girl in kaleidoscope shorts,
bright harlequin shorts, sitting in her mother's garden full of
bright nasturtiums climbing up the front door, and daisies the
colour of Porthcawl rock,
shocking pink and shocking blue and luminous green and
purple Livingstone daisies the colour of Teddy boys socks
opening in sunshine and closing in shadow, and hundreds of
china pink roses and bamboo that cuts the skin, and a sumac
tree on fire all through November.

*Song - "Moonlight becomes you, it goes with your hair
You certainly know the right things to wear."*

She wore swishy dresses
Swishy swishy dresses
And they whispered like the sea shore in the night.
Emerald green seamed silky stockings
Green metallic high heeled sling-backs
Broderie-anglaise backless sundress
Covered with red and purple lilies
Velvet coat and scent and chiffon
Petticoats and peeptoe shoes
Necklace, earrings, cigarettes
Oh her dresses were so swishy.
Swishy swishy swishy swishy
And she looks as though she's famous

She's a star, she's Ginger Rogers
With her smile, and dancing curls
Marlene Dietrich, Greta Garbo
With her hair and her high cheekbones
She's a beauty she's a flower
She looks just like Ginger Rogers
As she washes
Wrings out blankets
Beats the carpet, scrubs the floors
How she sings and how she dances
As she irons sheets at midnight.
She could be another woman
She could be someone else
On a silver screen in a darkened room
A darkened room that's full of strangers
She could be floating in the spotlight
She could be dancing in the dust
She could be another woman
But she wants to be herself
She just needs some inspiration
As she washes as she irons
And as she dusts and as she hoovers
She is dancing she is singing,
She is wearing swishy dresses
Swishy swishy swishy dresses
And they whisper like the seashore in the night
she sings "Moonlight becomes you, it goes with your hair."

Once upon a time there was a little girl sitting in her mother's garden, and her mother planted seeds and her mother planted flowers, and as her mother cwtched the flowers, cwtched them deep down in the earth, her mother told her stories, told her stories of her aunties, Aunty Dora who went to Canada to marry a Mounty and died giving birth to twins, Aunty Mimi who married a man because he had a steamroller, Aunty Mari who walked the mountains in the storms, Aunty Mary who went to Pennsylvania in 1926.

Song - "Now is the Hour for me to say Goodbye"

"Now is the hour for me to say goodbye,
Soon I'll be sailing far across the sea"

Leaving Pantyffynnon Station
Sailing out of Liverpool
Over the sea and over the ocean
Sailing over the far horizon
To Carbondale
she sings "America, America"
To find the promised land.
I have a veranda
In Pennsylvania
Fur coat and wireless,
A car in the garage,

A weekly massage,
I've been to Niagara, oh yes.
I'm swank and I'm posh
By golly, by gosh
I live in the promised land
In Carbondale
she sings "America America"
Far across the sea...

      the following is said in an American accent
Tomato potato tomato potato tomato potato
Tomato potato tomato - garage

Song - "Today I feel so happy"

"Today I feel so happy so happy happy
I don't know why I'm happy I only know I am."

Song - "When the roll is called up yonder"

"When the roll is called up yonder
When the roll is called up yonder I'll be there."

Aunty Hetty who played the tambourine
and preached on Gwaun-Cae-Gurwen square.

A voice like brown bread
Allinsons and wafer thin,

She cuts a slice for Jesus Christ
Who died for all her sins.
Jesus sits down at the table
Thin brown bread for Jesus,
Saves a sinner from his beer and fags
Loving him for Jesus.
Pray for a baby in the bedroom each night
Having sex for Jesus
Hetty and Wil in the bedroom all night
Making love, for Jesus
Saying their prayers,
There's three in the bed,
Hetty and Wil and Jesus Christ
Making love for Jesus.

Song - "I've heard of a land on a faraway strand"

Aunty Dora doing the everyday things
And laughing
Sitting on the windowsill
Far above the flowers
Outside the house
Looking in
Polishing the windows
Shaking her duster
And calling down "yo-hoo"
And laughing

Her smile like sunshine
Her face like the sun
Polishing the windows
Shaking her duster
Calling down
Outside the house
And laughing
Looking in
Looking in on the everyday things
Bread and tea and toasted cheese
Loosening her corset by candle-light
Shaking her duster
Polishing the windows
And laughing
Laughing and laughing
Laughing 'til she cries

Aunty Margaret, Aunty Margaret, Aunty Maggie
The third Margaret but the first one to live
Aunty Maggie joined the mission.

Song - *"When the trumpet of the Lord shall sound and time shall be no more."*

Far, far away in the middle of the mountains
The wild rocky craggy mountains
They are missionaries.

Aunty Maggie and her best friend Miss Cheyney
Buttoned up in their navy
In their bonnets and bows and gold rimmed specs,
They are missionaries.

Song - "With a nick nack paddywhack give a dog a bone."

They are saving the souls
That would otherwise burn
Their eyes on the cross
For paradise yearn
But the child with no shoes
And raggedy clothes
Runs and hides when they come
She's afraid of Miss Cheyney
And her friend Aunty Maggie
Buttoned up in their navy
Being missionaries
In Scotland.

Song- "And the trumpet of the Lord shall sound in Peebles, Stirling and Inverness..."

Aunty Jennie who came second
in the national five times.
My name is Jini
They call me Shini

And I sing
> *sings*

"tra la la la"
Oh my singing's like the ocean
Oh my singing's like the sea.
> *sings*

"Tra la la" and "tra la lee"
Operetta and Cantata
The Creation, The Messiah
> *sings*

"Haleliwia!"
The Eisteddfod, sacred concert
My eyes always smiling
My face always shining
I gargle with sherry
I swallow fresh eggs
I stand centre stage
And I wait for the quiet
And then when I'm ready
I let it escape.
It flies like a bird
Flying high in the sky
> *she sings the scales*

"Aaaaaaaaaaaaa!"
The notes are like silver
The applause is like gold.
And then there'll be flowers and tea in the vestry,

I talk and I laugh
I enjoy every minute
And then I go home in my little blue Ford
As I drive through the darkness
I see all the posters
Madame Jenny Evans Jones - Soprano.

And her mother played the piano for Aunty Jennie. She got her A.L.C.M. when she was 13. She was taught by a sadist, no playing comic songs, no music of the pictures.

Song - "Moonlight becomes you, it goes with your hair."

She never played the piano after she grew up.

What about the little flowers
Curled up tight inside?
They're so small
So very, very small,
Tiny, tiny, tiny
You've got to strain your eyes to see them
They're so tiny.
The little sweet flowers
The little shiny flowers
The little flowers inside.

Where do the talents go?

The little flowers inside,
All curled up tight inside.
Where are our mother's talents?
Out mother's mother's mother's?
All curled up tight inside
Deep down in the earth
The little flowers are cwtshing,
They go from womb to womb,
Waiting, waiting waiting.

One day
What if they escaped?
What if they burst out
In all their glory,
Water lily, valley lily
Purple lily, yellow lily.
What if they burst out
When no-one is looking
When everyone is busy
Doing something else?
What if the flowers burst out?
Waterfalls of roses
A storm of lovely lilies
Millions of petals
Showers of soft petals
Falling on the world,
Everything will change then

Old roads will disappear
We'll have to find some new roads
To find our way back home.
Waterfalls of roses
Storms of lovely lilies,
Millions of them.

And the little girl always took her mother flowers, snowdrops, snowflowers, snowjewels, the first little white lilies to push their heads through the snow by the stream by the house.

Song - "O lili wen fach, o ble daethost ti"
     she hums it for two lines

And armfuls of bluebells from the graveyard in the spring.

As soon as she shot out of the water
Like a perfect rubber dolly
With her skin a purply colour
And her arms and legs were bouncing
And her small strong voice was calling
Oh so clearly, so determined.
As soon as she shout out of the water
Her mother's womb filled with fear,
A terrible fear,
Fear the size of a house
Fear the size of a giant,

Fear of losing her little angel
Her sweet flower
Her gem, her diamond, her pearl
Her treasure
Her beautiful fruit, her perfection.
Afraid of the stillness of the surface of the lake
Afraid it would be smooth and quiet again.
Without her murmur, without her laughter
Without her shouting, without her screaming
Rippling the water
Whirling the water.

The drops, the colours of the rainbow
Red and yellow and purple and green
And blue and orange
The colours of the rainbow
Wetting her all over,
Because of all the colours
Because of the fear of losing the colours
And having to live in a black and white world
She had to be careful.
You can't have a bathing suit
In case you drown
You can't have a chiffon frock
In case you dance,
You can't have high heels
In case you fall

You can't have silk stockings
You can't paint your face
Jezebel, Delilah
You can't be a woman in case.
Because of in case
She crept in her slippers,
Walked on her tiptoes
Hid behind the bushes
To peep, to spy.
Just in case.
The door must be closed
The door must be locked
And the key must be hidden
In case my little angel
My sweet flower
My gem, my diamond, my pearl
My treasure
My beautiful fruit, my perfection
The prettiest princess in the world
Runs away and gets hurt,
In case the toy breaks.
And the rag doll lies on the floor
White as a sheet, no colour in her cheeks
Every drop of blood's been sucked
Her empty eyes staring at the window
The frame is nailed down tight.

Now I lay me down to sleep
Pray the Lord my soul to keep
If I die before I wake
Pray the Lord my soul to take.

*Song - "Ring a ring of roses, a pocket full of posies
Atishhoo, atishoo we all fall down."*

Fie for shame, fie for shame turn your backs to the wall again.

*Song - "Wallflowers, wallflowers, climbing up so high
We're all pretty children and we all must die"*

And then the little girl watches her mother digging the garden carrying the earth in a wheelbarrow in a chiffon dress and long velvet gloves, and the little girl watches her mother cutting coal in high heels and silk stockings with seams and carrying water from the well in a big black hat with a spotted veil and no-one could see her.

It was just a bit of fun
With her boyfriend on the mountain,
Playing about on top of the mountain,
Just playing about
The starry stars were twinkling like
Diamonds in the vast and endless
Deep blue heaven

And the full shiny moon was glowing
In its hazy rainbow ring.
It was nice on top of the mountain
The heather was like purple velvet
Like a purple velvet carpet
She started to take off her clothes
And threw them carelessly
on the heather
Just for fun
Just playing about
She started running
And her clothes went up in the air
And fell it didn't matter where
In bright patches in the moonlight
She was laughing
And throwing her clothes carelessly
On the heather
The clothes she didn't want, she didn't want,
She didn't want
The chapel coat, the coat of lies
The hypocritical hat
The scarf that suffocates
The Pharisaical frock
The boots that betray, the Sunday school stockings of slavery.

She was bursting her buttons
Peeling perilously

Doing the starlight striptease
The wild waltz of freedom
And the sheep watched with dead eyes
And the sheep could see.
She was running and running
Running faster
Running further
Faster than every before
Further than ever before
As fast as she can
Her chest is tight
Her breath is short
The heather is scratching her feet
And her feet have started to bleed
But the mountain top is endless
She can't get to Carreg Cennen
She can't get to Llygad Llwchwr
And sail away on a boat of leaves to sea.
She runs and runs
Faster and faster in the moonlight
Further and further in the starlight
But the mountain top is endless.

Once upon a time, long long ago the little girl in a frilly pink dress, in a shiny smudgy dress, in kaleidoscope shorts sitting sometimes in her grandmother's garden and sometimes in her mother's garden in the middle of the flowers seeing them open and close and studying the shape of the leaves and their petals, looking into the depths of their souls to eternity and trying to climb into them. Seeing the seeds grown into plants so she can climb up on their branches into the clouds.

And the little girl took her mother's flowers, snowdrops, bluebells. And her mother had no electricity and wrung heavy blankets by hand and she ran on the mountain, and her garden was full of Meri and Mari and butterflies, and her grandmother made Welsh cakes and ginger beer and worked in the tin works and took in washing for threepence and sang on the mountain and grew purple pom-poms and dahlias and yellow Easter daisies. And her great grandmother polished shoes under the cherry tree, polished shoes 'til they sparkled, only 14 pairs of shoes, under the cherry tree, and her great, great grandmother bled to death at the side of the road on the way to work in the candle factory. And her mother wore swishy swishy dresses and emerald green stockings, and went dancing and to the pictures and wrung out heavy blankets by hand, and her grandmother worked in the tin works and knitted socks and rode a bike with her feet on the handlebars and whistled as she turned the Welsh cakes.

Sweet fragment of memory
Stitched together like the petals
Of ragged roses
Dancing in the wind

Before flying down the rivers of my dreams.

Song - "Hiraeth"

"Dwedwch fawrion o wybodaeth
O ba beth y gwnaethpwyd hiraeth,
A pa ddefnydd a rhoid ynddo
Na ddarfyddai wrth ei wishgo.

Derfydd aur a derfydd arian
Derfydd melfed, derfydd shidan.
Derfydd pob dilledyn helaeth
Ond er hyn ni dderfydd hiraeth.

Hiraeth mawr a hiraeth creulon
Hiraeth sydd yn torri 'nghalon.
Pan fwyf dryma'r nos yn cysgu
Fe ddaw hiraeth ac am defry.

Hiraeth, hiraeth, cilia, cilia,
Paid â phwyso mor drwm arna'i.
Nesa dipyn at yr erchwyn
Gad i mi gael cysgu gronyn."

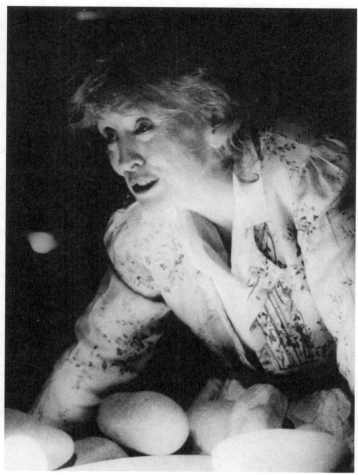

Sharon Morgan, Magic Threads 1997   Photo: Brian Tarr

CHRISTINE WATKINS

Christine Watkins was born in New Inn, Gwent, and educated at Stanwell Comprehensive School, Penarth, and graduated in Drama & English at the University of Wales, Aberystwyth, in 1979. In 1981 she co-founded Cwmni Cyfri Tri, and she has worked extensively with theatre companies in Wales and beyond. In 1989 she adapted Charlotte Perkin Gilman's *The Yellow Wallpaper (Y Papur ar y Pared)* for Hwyl a Fflag. Made in Wales Stage Company performed *Adult Ways* in 1986, the 'Write On!' festival in 1994 featured a rehearsed reading of *The Mother House*, and the Company performed *The Sea that Blazed* in 1996 and *Queen of Hearts* in 1998. A cabaret play, *Hocus Pocus* (New Theatre Works), and *Rosa*, an outdoor music-theatre piece (Feel Good Theatre Productions), were performed in 2000.

Her television work includes *Oed yr Addewid (Homing)* for Red Rooster Films in 1986. BBC Radio Wales broadcast her play *Home from the Dance* in 1989, and in 1993 she co-wrote *Anchoress*, a feature film commissioned by the British Film Institute. She has written a libretto, *Black February (Mis Bach Du)*, for Welsh National Opera (1997), and is currently working on a studio play, a site-specific play and a performed/recorded text in collaboration with three visual artists.

She has been a Lecturer in Drama at the University of Wales, Aberystwyth, and at the University of Wales, Bangor, and she has also taught several creative writing courses.

WELCOME TO MY WORLD

Welcome to My World was premièred at 'Performing Words', a residential workshop run by the Magdalena Project at Elan Valley, Powys, February 1998.

Ada	Christine Watkins
Second Performer	Geddy Aniksdal
	(Grenland Friteater, Norway)

QUEEN OF HEARTS

Queen of Hearts was premièred at the Sherman Theatre, Cardiff, May/June 1998. (One of the characters was eighty-two year old Annie, the speaker of the following monologue.)

Annie	Jenny Hill
Director	Jeff Teare

Christine Watkins

Welcome to my World

Music : Jim Reeves, 'This World is not my home'

ADA is sat at a table sorting through piles of records, cassettes and a very few personal effects, including an old piano accordion. Also on the table are several empty Benedictine bottles. ADA's finger has got plasters on it from being cut with a knife. Next to the table is a bin bag, into which she drops an odd item now and then.

She switches off the cassette; the music breaks off abruptly. She listens.

ADA

...Shoona?

Nothing. She switches the cassette back on again and continues sorting out until the track ends. Then she switches off the cassette abruptly, ejects the cassette and chucks it straight in the bin.

I know what you're looking at...

I'm usually very deft with a kitchen knife. I can do waterlily tomatoes without any of those plastic gadgets...

Definitely not a case of like mother like daughter, because she was always a very haphazard chopper, even when she was lucid. Especially when she was lucid... It's a wonder she had any digits left - slicing a carrot nearly had irreversible consequences on more than one occasion.

Obviously it's been a while since she had any access to knives.

She told them in the home that her single bedded room was in fact the Hall of the great goddess Freya. And the corridor outside was the realm of ice and blizzards which they traversed at their peril.

I'd seen it coming from a long way off. The great goddess Freya had been creeping into conversation for a long time but I'd always managed to ward her off; the same with several other deities of the frozen tundra or the spring forest, depending on the mood. Frozen tundra gained the upper hand in the end though. The Black Ice bear was coming she said, and I thought, I know where that's leading.

Water off a duck's back to the regular staff of course. Still, some of the Saturday girls became understandably distressed by insistence on remaining naked at all times except for a string of diamonds.

I said, that's nothing!

Not real diamonds of course. Glass. She bought them in David Morgan's years ago.

I said you should see how *I* found her sometimes! Never knew what I was going to see when I opened that door. That's if I *could* open it. One time I stood outside here struggling for twenty minutes and I thought, what's stopping it? It can't be unpaid phone bills, she hasn't got a phone. Is it a chair?

Leaves. That's what it was. *Deliberately* piled up in a drift inside and stuck in the door jamb.

They said "Was that type of thing a regular occurence?" I said I didn't visit regularly, we had an understanding.

There was some rubbish in the wardrobe, mind! Most of it went straight on the back of the fire. And that fur coat... Huge old thing. At first glance I thought; I don't want to have to find houseroom for it - take it to the Heart Foundation shop. But then I looked closer. Stained and soiled...dragged through a hedge backwards would be an understatement. So I thought I'll cut it up, manoeuvre the bits into a bin bag and that'll be that. Gone.

...It's all going, anyway.

she shoves a few old LPs into the bag

I'm not an anything goes person when it comes to church ceremonial. But the last note she wrote this side of coherence said very clearly in capital letters "JIM's NOT HYMNS". I told the organist my hands were morally tied, he seemed quite alright about it. I said to keep the muffle on.

She pops an unmarked cassette into the player. ADIOS AMIGO fills the room.

Yes, you said it, Jimbo.

She leaves the track play as she sorts a few more objects into the bin bag, then she ejects the cassette and chucks that away too.

Anyway we didn't sing. Even if you'd been there we wouldn't have sung. It wasn't appropriate...

You'd have realised that, Shoona, had you been present. Still, as you were *not* present... as you were - a day late ? Oh, a little more than that I think, don't you. A little more than a day!

What did you do, did you walk all the way from Tromso...?

As you were not present you'll have to take my word for it.
I didn't have people back here afterwards. I didn't want people
trekking up here poking their noses in. Time for a thorough
clear out on my own. As I thought...

***

I don't look like you remember, do I?

You'll have to excuse me for that, of course, since in the normal
run of things a few bodily changes do tend to occur between the
ages of six and forty one...

- Yes, that's it, you try going outside to the toilet and you'll
bang your nose right into your face! That wall was blocked up
years ago. She had the bathroom extension built in 1970. And
due to my putting my foot down she had it refitted in Avocado
in 82 and again last year in Champagne.

There's a guest towel there... there's always one there... for
eventualities.

I should warn you that the flush is not quite as it should be. I
recently had cause to remove this from the cistern.

She picks up an empty bottle of Benedictine from the floor and puts it next to the others on the table.

She maintained it was made by nuns, I said I think you'll find it's made by Monsanto.

...Cistern, I said.

Not sister.

It's a plumbing term - I've no idea what it is in Norwegian.

Still, the kitchen hasn't altered much has it? Not at all. You see she was resistant to change in here, despite my best efforts.

This is where she stood, just here, with the knife raised... and lowered... raised and lowered, chop, chop, chopping.

And here... there was always a big tin of plasters here, wasn't there?

ADA gets the tin of plasters out of a cupboard and bangs it down on the worksurface.

Da-daaaaa! How about that?

What a life you must have led, away from it all ! I can't begin to imagine it! And a university degree in Glacier Mechanics! It's a far cry from Llanddewi Infants, isn't it? Still you weren't there more than a month were you. I don't s'pose you even remember it do you? The pair of us walking to school like this...

She stretches out her hand as if to hold another hand.

No, don't try and tell me you remember.

Mind you it's amazing what you absorb at a very young age isn't it? Of course the rest of the kids were busy learning Humpty Dumpty sat on a wall - whereas I went to school word perfect on Distant Drums, He'll have to go and I Look Around And There's a Heartache Following Me.

She sits back down to her task.

I'm working through it all systematically.

...Of course she could have died here if she'd made the effort.

***

She is about to put a stack of tapes in the bin; she stops and peers at one.
 Yes, it really is. Oh yes, I assure you.

She puts the cassette on:
Music: 'Make the world go away'
She listens for a while as she sorts, then switches it off

Well as you're here... I suppose you'd better stay the night.
Unless you've made other arrangements. In fact I'd better stay
as well. Yes I think that would be best.

It's not a problem just for one night - anyway it wouldn't seem
right to leave you here alone.

I don't have to show you the way, surely. It's perfectly alright -
the bed is made up.

I came in to see to a few things before the funeral, I didn't see
any need to leave the place looking as if no one had bothered.
A sleeping bag will not be necessary.

No, not even a very good quality sleeping bag. 1000 kroner.
Four seasons, microfibre, lightweight, suitable for Arctic
conditions...

Yes well you won't find Arctic conditions around Builth Wells
in May not even in a bad year. There's linen pressed and aired.
Don't keep on about things. You still keep on about things
don't you?

Remember that song you used to keep on about? You know what song I mean - the one about the man caught in a storm. I used to have to say Mam switch it off now or she'll keep on about it all day.

Switch it off, switch it off...

He was caught in the snow on his way back home to his love. What was her name now... Mary Ann. Mary Ann, that's it. There was a blizzard wrapped around her house.

"Yes, they found him there on the plains, his hands froze to the reins, He was just a hundred yards from Mary Ann..."

She starts to look half-heartedly for the song

It's here somewhere...

She gets up. She touches the piano accordion, which gives out an eerie sound

She never taught me to play. Or you, did she.

Are you thinking about one night in particular? *I'm* not.
I'm not thinking about any night at all, never mind any night in particular.

Nights without any light, only the white of the snow at the window - oh, we were always having power cuts, nothing unusual in that.

That night - if it *was* any particular night, I mean... we were playing Ludo.

No lights, only the paraffin lamp. We sat by the window so that we could take advantage of the moonlight reflecting off the snow...

Glittering white... or as you might say, 'glitrende hvitt'...

You started crying because you couldn't get a six to start... and Mam said she'd give you one of her sixes, which I didn't really think was fair.

...And then you ran out, didn't you. And that was that! Gone. I'd never have brought it up, mind, but since you have brought it up well there we are!

I mean you have the gall to breeze in here after thirty five years, wearing snowshoes, with no word of explanation or apology, too late for the funeral -

I have no desire to see your passport. I didn't say I didn't believe you.

I'm not coming up straight away, I want to carry on. You go on, make yourself at home...

... D'you know what I think?

I think you carry that night with you. I think you carry it with you in a little box, wherever you go, and every now and then you take it out and look at it... And you open up the little lid... and you see her in that night in that box, looking up at the window and seeing something... She's seeing a dark, dark shape - better close the lid quick!

...Open it up again just a tiny bit... and there's a small tinkling voice... like the sound of little bells coming from far away, saying...We must all go to bed at once and not take any notice of that shape at the window. Come along girls...

You've brought it with you, haven't you, that little box. You've probably got it with you in your bag at this very moment!

Well fortunately it holds no fears for me, because I've got no memory of anything at all like that! In fact, it's probably a Norwegian folk tale, there's lots of those aren't there? That's what it is. Myths of the Norsemen.

... Still there? Go on, off you go to bed, you must be tired after such a long journey...

I've got things I want to finish, here in the kitchen...

Lights begin to fade down; track fades up: 'Goodnight Irene'...
Track fades down

You never went to bed that night did you? You sat and watched from the tops of the stairs...

...and downstairs the door opened.

I know what you think you saw.

The dark shape... the huge dark shape of a bear...

But there was no such thing !

Don't you tell me there *was* such a thing!

I hid my head under the blankets, as instructed. And you sat and saw the bear come right inside the house! It was almost completely dark... black, black night in the house... You felt your way downstairs... the bear was in here, in this kitchen... You followed it outside to where the sky was full of snow and stars ... you followed it out of this dark kitchen, out through the snow...and he lifted you up and carried you right away from the house. And he gave you meat and honey and berries on little plates of leaves...

He wrapped you up warm. You can still remember the smell of his fur and his breath and his skin. Can you?

Is that it?

Is it?!

We looked for you for days, they said no child could have survived out in that!

Oh yes, they said, that's given their mother something to really cry about now, they said You never know, perhaps that'll sober her up!

Well I have two things I want to say.

One, a four year old child cannot be kept alive by a bear; not as far as I'm concerned.

And two, there are no bears around here anyway!

It's time to go to bed now. Yes, I'm coming...

After a pause
Goodnight Irene...

Another pause
Irene goodnight...

TRACK fades up again, fainter than before, from where it left off. 'Goodnight Irene'
ADA looks out of the window. It is snowing thickly. She turns away in fear.

She musters the courage to look again. No snow.

ADA looks at a small box on the floor. From the top a furry arm trails. ADA dares to investigate. A long fur coat. ADA puts it on.

As 'Goodnight Irene' fades down

Is this what you've come back for?

Well it's very resistant to knives, I can tell you that much. She was keeping it...

...How can you be so sure she wanted you to have it? There was no will, I can tell you that now, because there was nothing to leave! Only beads, and they're glass.
...It's stained and soiled... Did she write to you and tell you to come for it?

You can see it, can't you... her standing there crying. Oh yes, she was a great crier. Sob sob chop chop sob sob. Sobs reach a certain point, quick tinkle on the piano accordion, feel a bit better. Welcome to my world.

I've seen it a million times, her standing there crying. Never asked her why. Oh, a thousand terrifying reasons, coming in from the cold and dark, outside the kitchen door! Don't tell me I could have asked her, because you could have asked her!

Ask her now if you're so worried about it, but I don't want to. No I do not.

I'm going to bed. You can't make things better for people once they're dead. I don't want to sit here with you and light a candle and ask her why she was crying, I don't want to join in that kind of rubbish. I don't want to sit here waiting for no answer.

*****

Track: 'Blue Skies'
Bright morning light.

She walked into a Jim Reeves album and couldn't find her way out again, that's why she was crying!
She continues the clean up

Of course, the great goddess Freya is the goddess of love. Well, love and various other things. She decorated the walls of her great hall with the contents of her makeup bag, very much in the style of those caves in France. They'd tried to remove the traces, but lipstick is not the easiest substance to remove from flock wallpaper. They were still spraying and rubbing when I got there. I said "Well... ?" She said the walls were bare, I've painted on them with ochre.

It was too. Ochre Desire, Max Factor.

They'd very kindly provided her with headphones, and I offered to take the tapes in, as many as she wanted, but no. She didn't want Jim in there, she said. She preferred to think of him waiting safe and sound for her in the house. Well I think she just didn't like the headphones. Anyway I didn't push it. She did say on a few occasions that she wanted the piano accordion brought in - but I thought of the staff. Oh, there were tears, but I said to her, now come on, think it through. The great goddess Freya wouldn't have bothered with piano accordions. She'd have had wind chimes and rattling reindeers bones and ...well, that type of thing.

That's right isn't it? Instruments of the snow and ice - you'd know about that wouldn't you?

No, she'd lost all track of day and night, and the sound carries.

It wouldn't have been fair.

D'you know one of the Saturday girls said to me... "I hope you don't mind me saying, but she seems a little bit afraid of you..." Afraid of me! I was the last thing she had to be afraid of! I kept it all at bay, I did! *I* didn't run away.

I don't think I'm up to providing a typically Norwegian breakfast but perhaps you'd settle for a light omelette...?

You always used to say "Switch it off Mami!"when that song came on, didn't you. It wasn't me who wanted it switched off! I only wanted it switched of because of you!

I know what she said - I remember what she said when you woke up crying in the night.

She said, don't worry, because there's another song on the B-side...another version of the same song. And in that version the man *does* get home to Mary Ann! Because Mary Ann comes out with a light, to meet him, you see, and he sees her light shining and he fixes his eyes on it and he's guided the last hundred yards back to the warmth and safety of the house...
That's what she used to tell you, wasn't it? Am I right?

Well the time has come for me to disabuse you of that comforting notion, because there was no such B side. Look, it's bound to be here somewhere, I'll prove it...

She rifles through the stuff for a moment

And as a matter of fact, just for the record, it was the horse dying that always got me.

Didn't you realize? ...Didn't you realize he was riding a horse? Of course he was... Otherwise how could his hands be froze to the reins?

...Yes, sad isn't it. That's given you something to cry about now, hasn't it.

Him and his horse lying there... I expect you can picture it all too well, can't you? Not dismembered, mind. There was nothing dismembered about him. Just dead. Exposure, I expect.

Lying there in the soft powdery snow that follows after a blizzard...

Extensive frostbite would be certain at that temperature, that's what everybody said. You'd know all about that, wouldn't you... what with you being a professor of snow...

And eventually, as sure as night follows day... Black specks in the sky - crows coming to peck out his eyes...

And his horse's eyes.

Yes, it has to be said. His horse's eyes as well.

... She died in bed at half past three in the morning. Since you ask.

I wasn't there but I'm told it was all quite quiet.

I hear you... I hear you Shoona, perfectly well, but I don't understand what you're saying. Because I really don't understand a word of your language - well, it's not really your language though, is it? Your adopted tongue let's say.

Could you by any chance be saying that you're sorry you didn't contact me... Or her? In all these years? Is that what you've come to say?

I think I know what it was.

She picks up a bottle and puts her finger on hers lips in warning

She said "Fingers on lips, don't say a word, because it's none of their bloody business!"

And you just got into the habit of keeping quiet, that's what it was. Then you couldn't stop keeping quiet, could you? Quiet as ice...

- You look very cold to me, Shoona. You're not cold are you? You certainly shouldn't be cold you know. Not on a fine day like this. The second day of the lovely month of May.

It's very like a day I was thinking about. A particular day...

Of course, I can remember back before you were born, or thought of. It's like a kind of key I hold, I suppose. The key to a little box.

That day, you know, was a day in May, bright and clear, very much like today. She took me out walking here in the beautiful environs of Builth Wells, right out in amongst the trees... When I was tiny, it was. I was only three, I must have only been three... Miles and miles to walk, it was. Bearing in mind that things seem further when you're small...

She went on ahead, and she disappeared into the mouth of a great big cave. I struggled on after her. She was sitting inside on a rock and she couldn't get up. And do you know what, it started to snow. Just April snow, a few days late... I don't think she could focus. She managed to light a fire though. I picked up the sticks... Then she lay down. We stayed there all night. And in the night - in the night, Shoona, I must have had a dream or something, because I saw a big black shape in the mouth of the cave...

You have unusual dreams at home, don't you. I can see you standing there under the Northern Lights, having very remarkable dreams...

Well the funny thing is I don't think this was a dream, because I shut my eyes tight but every time I peeped it was still there.

It was just like a bear, coming in out of the snow. A Black Ice Bear... I remember its shape and its shadow moving moving on the wall... curling itself around her, again and again, moving across the wall, and she was making little moans...

And then in the New Year you were born.

Just a tiny little thing you were when you were born. Tiny, but very very fierce.

There you are you see!

You said there was a bear, well there was! You insisted on it! He wrapped the whole world in a blizzard!

But what I would like to take this opportunity to ask is, you were four years old, how could you run out like that into the snow in your nightie!

You didn't have to go so far! All that way, all the way past the realm of ice and blizzards which we traverse at our peril.

...Out of character to go off like that without me. That's what they said.

That's what they said, Shoona!

And then never ever again a word or sight of Shoona!

Out of character, to go off and leave... me...with her.

***

Of course, they said, of course she shouldn't be allowed to keep the older one, but you want to watch her because she'll scream and lash out if anyone tries to take her away, she'll scream and lash out like a wild creature...

She stuffs the fur coat into a binbag and sits down at the table again, which is now almost clear

***

No. Don't come back. It's too far. Anyway I've nearly finished the clearing out. She didn't need all this stuff any more anyway. She'd whittled it right down to glass beads and Ochre Desire...

I could visit the Northern Lights some time. I understand they're very spectacular. I could stand there under the same cold sky as you... with the Great Bear who keeps the heavens turning in due season...

I wanted her to die here. That's what I wanted. But this house is not suitable for someone who has discovered that they're the great goddess Freya.

... She always liked to have all the lights on in the house. That's how she liked to listen to music. In the kitchen with all the lights on. Sob sob, chop chop... Feeling better? Welcome to my world...

Music plays: 'Welcome to my World'.

Christine Watkins 1999.

About the monologues

Queen of Hearts was commissioned by Made in Wales, and performed in the Sherman Theatre, Cardiff in May/June 1998 as a full length play with four characters, one of whom was eighty-two year old ANNIE, who features in the monologue.

The play as performed in full followed the relationships of three of the characters, including ANNIE, with SYLVIA, a former professional Princess of Wales lookalike. The original production had a controversial journey to the stage, as the play was first commissioned and written *prior* to the death of the Princess of Wales, and the decision to continue involved much thought and discussion, re-drafts, articles in Big Issue, etc. all of which made it quite a hot project to see through.

Now, at a little distance, I have chosen to present the character of ANNIE here in monologue form, mainly because her robust take on the strange, obsessive world she is locked into was a joy to work on - and also because I think she's a great vehicle for an older female actor.

ANNIE in the original Made in Wales production was played by Jennifer Hill.

I developed *Welcome to My World* in a Performing Words residential workshop run by the Magdalena Project in February 1998, (Elan Valley, Powys) where it was given its first presentation, with myself playing the role of ADA. That presentation was given with the assistance of Geddy Aniksdal of

Grenland Friteater, Norway, as a second performer; *Welcome to My World* has since continued in development as a bilingual piece (English/Norwegian) but is presented here in English voice only.

It reflects my interest in combining differing elements in the creation of a piece of text for performance, in this case taking the music of Jim Reeves as its starting point and spanning naturalistic and stylized speech forms and performance modes in the exploration of a memory.

Christine Watkins. November 1999

Christine Watkins & Jeff Teare, Queen of Hearts, May 1998
Photo: Brian Tarr

adapted extract from

Queen of Hearts

ANNIE is seated on a park bench.

ANNIE

That was the beginning of the end with Raye, obsessions and fantasies. Diana staring out from every wall... I said, "it's about time we had a new face to look at. Marlene Dietrich or someone."

Anything would set him off. I borrowed one of his souvenir t-shirts - well, I was cold in the night, I only had a thin nightie!! Then in the morning I thought, I'll just pop it under the mattress. Not hiding it, just keeping it flat so he wouldn't have to iron it. Well, if I did...

Took my bag and off out for the day, that was the only answer. Course he had to have a good look, I said, "it's not your bag, Raye, it's mine! What's the matter, can't I go out of the room now without being frisked?"

Anyway there was nothing in it, only a few seedlings, that's all.

I dug two yards or metres and no one had taken any notice so I thought, right, these are going in. I wanted Kohl Rabi but they only had Little Gems...

Course, he was off. "What do *you* want seedlings for?" I said, "ah, it's in us all somewhere. My granny used to say "the earth is in our blood" - and she was one hundred and three years of age when she died."

He said, "Well Annie you're only 82, you've got your whole life in front of you!"

I don't want my whole life in front of me thank you very much, I want it behind me where it belongs. But I thought, these may live on after I am gone... things I've planted in my last days. I knew it was the right spot, just under the chestnut trees...it's out of the way and there's a specal sort of light...

I had it indicated to me, you see. There was a special kind of luminous shape there on one occasion. Like a form, in the light... foretelling. Foretelling that my end may be soon...

He said "Oh, seeing angels now are we?"

Now, I can accept obsessions and fantasies, up to a point but cynicism I cannot tolerate. I said, "I never said angels, I never said that! A luminous shape, I said...!"

Should have kept my mouth shut.

"Come out for a stroll Raye," I said, "come and help me make the desert bloom," I said to him on more than one occasion....

You wouldn't get him out of that room, you wouldn't get him to leave all his posters and souvenir bloody t shirts!

I said, "you've got to drop all this sooner or later Raye. It's gone too far, it's crossed the line. They'll have you out of here any excuse!"

He said, "You don't know anything about angels, you don't know the first thing!"

I slipped out of there quick, while he had his back to the door.

...Off to my chestnut trees. Bag of seedlings, bag of slug pellets.

Course I didn't realize I was going to be faced with the living dead looming up out of the mist! Her with all that gear and the look on her face...

She said, "Oh, I'm so sorry, have I upset you?"

- I said, "never mind about upsetting *me*, there's all sorts walk through this park. It would only take one who wasn't mentally robust and it could just push them over the edge, seeing you there, all got up like that." She said, "oh I can't help it, it's just a natural likeness. I did used to do this professionally, but I gave that up *of course* ."

I thought, well this is out of the frying pan into the bloody fire.

Her sat there... with the leaves all around her... looking like a photograph... I thought, it'll be me getting obsessions and fantasies at this rate.

I said, "bugger off."

She didn't budge though.

She said, "Little Gems, I see. They'll need more sunlight, it's shady here under the trees..." I said, "they'll have to take their chances, same as the rest of us."

She said "I don't think slug pellets are a good idea in a public setting. Still," she said, *"this is a very special spot isn't it?"*

"Is it?" I said, "Oh yes," she said, "Once I thought I saw something very special just in this spot, not a face or a figure or anything like that, but something!"

That's what got me.

Her sat there, looking like a ghost, saying that. It got me for a minute.

And I said, "that's it! That's like I saw, clear as daylight ! Not a face, not a figure, but something!"

...She said, "Well I'm sorry if I startled you".

I said, "if Raye saw you now he'd either be thrilled or he'd go right off his trolley."

- She said, "who's Raye?"

*****

He was sat there, when I got back, room all in darkness, candles under all the posters.

He had the wardrobe open, always a bad sign. I thought, that dress'll be out... and it was. It's an exact copy. Emmanuel, all the trimmings. God knows where he got it. It took up the whole wardrobe. Where I'm meant to put my personal effects is immaterial!

He was sat there like that with all the candles and the fire
hazard and all, and he turned to me and he said "Annie, she
was the loneliest person in the world...!"

I mean, why the hell should *she* have to be the loneliest person
in the world? Why shouldn't someone in a bedsit in
Aberbargoed be the loneliest person in the world?!

I said, "look....even if she had come here, what d'you think
would have happened - you think your eyes would have met, do
you, I said. Your eyes would have met across a crowded room
and she'd have fallen in love with you... Well, I'm sorry to have
to tell you they're trained to avoid eye contact, like sniffer
dogs."

He said, "you don't have to pin it down, you don't have to
make it sound stupid!"

And he sat there then, all crestfallen.
I thought right, take the bull by the horns, because we're getting
nowhere here.

So I said, "Listen Raye... I saw someone today. Someone in the
park. it was someone you might like to meet. You see, if you
met this person, and you know, had a bit of a chat, you might
be inspired to - well to get out and start getting on with things

again. Because you were doing well Raye, you were. And I'm telling you, they'll have you out of here if they think you can't cope with the demands. No two ways about that. If they think you can't cope with everyday life! Doing things, doing your chores..."

I said to him, "we're a team aren't we Raye. We're comfortable, we're set up here - we don't want to spoil things."

He said, "I can't stand it when you go out, Annie... I can't get to sleep if you're not here."

I said, "I'm here now Raye, so you can get off to sleep any time you like.

We're getting there, Raye...we're getting there. That's teamwork, you see..."

Didn't get out of the room for over a week after that, only to the toilet.

***

Course by the time I got back here there was nothing left of my Little Gems above ground level, only stumps! I said if I set eyes on her again I'll give her slug pellets in a public place!

Course I turned round and there she was. Just stood there. As if she was waiting or something...

I said, "do you think she was the nearest thing to an angel on earth?"

She said, "oh no. No, I don't think so." I said, "well Raye does. Course, he's only twenty three. We share a room. It's not allowed strictly speaking, but he dresses like a woman so nobody says anything."

That shut her up.

She said, "Well I must say you're a jolly good advert for ageing." I said, "ah, keep branching out in new directions, that's the secret. I applied for a women's computer course the other week, only they said no over sixty fives. Apparently gender is immaterial after that."

She said, "oh yes, there's possibilities for success in every direction! Sometimes you can leave the past behind and see an open door in front of you and just bound through it!"

She had nice hands... a bit on the big side but very well manicured - of course they'd have to be for all the handshaking she had to do in her professional capacity. I got hold of one, I said, "you don't mind do you." She didn't pull away. I said, "I see this is a very special hand. I don't always sense that. D'you know the first thing that strikes me about this hand? Confusion. You see the pattern of our lives is set out in the heavenly realms, that's the stars and so forth and reflected in our palms *but* - it's what we do with the pattern that counts. So I look at the happiness here plain as daylight in your hand and I compare it with the aura of unhappiness that surrounds you..."

Ah, I looked at her face and I knew I'd touched the spot. She said, "Ooh I don't think I'm surrounded with an aura of unhappiness am I?"

"Oh, yes. And when I see that enormous contrast I say, your happy hand has got confused with someone else's tragic destiny."

Course she huffed and puffed and she wouldn't have it. She said, "oh, people always think that but I'm not at all confused. Never. There has never been any confusion of that sort for me, it was just a job that's all. I just took advantage of certain similarities of a purely physical nature."

I said, "you're what we call in denial. The lines cannot lie. Your true self is an as yet undiscovered country."

"Come and meet Raye," I said.

"I would bring him here to meet you but he's a bit of a homebird. A bit housebound, as you might say. It's all connected. I've tried to ignore it as the months have gone by, but it's no good. It's an infatuation you see, an obsession.

And they'll have him out of there, you see, if he carries on.

But if Raye was to meet you...

Well, who knows, you might be able to shift something, you might be able to bring him back to his senses! And then you see, in the process of helping a poor struggling fellow being, *you might find yourself once again in tune with your own happy destiny...*"

Of course she wanted to know all the details, life lines and so on, so I said, "oh the hands don't show all the ways and means it's just a rough guide..."

I said, "it'll have to be handled sensitively of course, I'll see to all that. I'll make the arrangements and let you know."

I said, "I'll meet you here then shall I?... I'll see you here again, in this special place..."

She said, "Oh yes... once when I was sat here I really thought I saw... a way forward."

I said, "was that when you saw the luminous shape...?"

She said, "what luminous shape...?"

I said, "that's what you told me. Not a face, not a form, a shape in the light!"

She said, "Oh no, no. That was nothing at all really. Of course there's always patches of light under the trees, you must have seen them. A sort of dappled effect... but it's nothing really."

"Ay... That's right," I said. "Nothing really. Bloody trees that's all. Dappled effect... Nothing special at all, not really..."

***

He was like a coiled spring. I could tell that straight away.

I said to him, "this woman who's going to visit you Raye... she seems a very nice person. Very nice indeed. And she's had a lot to put up with - worse than you in a way, because she was - close to her, you know. Like a shadow. And when she visits - well, it'll be just like what might have been Raye! The pair of you can sit down, take your time, talk it through, have a cup of tea... then you can start to put it all behind you.

And then we can settle down again, get back to normal, back on an even keel! What d'you think? I said, Because I've had a bit of a rethink Raye. My end may not be soon after all. And there's no such things as angels Raye. No, there isn't. And sometimes what you think is a portent may just be a trick of the light..."

He never answered. He just took the dress out of the wardrobe and put it on. He looked like a duvet.

I said, "I've done my best with you Raye but you don't try! You just want to mess around with all this Lady bloody Princess stuff, you're not normal!" He said, "I am normal! I'm like millions of people all over the planet who are truly fascinated by a truly fascinating woman!" I said, "*were* fascinated. *Were!* Anyway there's fascinated and there's obsessed - and *you* are obsessed."

He said, "Well at least I'm not a shagged out old whore who's staggered on bloody thirty years too long!"

I said, "I'm a grandmother figure and everybody loves me."

He said, "I don't fucking love you!"

***

I can take a beating, mind. I haven't got where I am without -

She breaks off shakily

...But those flats are reconstructed family-style units! I said I'd share with him, no one else wanted to share with him, no one else wanted to share with a bloody transvestite!

I came from there, I didn't even bring my coat.

He said, "Annie, you're not going to ask to have me moved are you? I mean we're used to one another now," he said. "You don't want to change now..."

I said, "I don't want to, Raye, because it's not convenient. But I've got to review my options now Raye, I said. Because there's possibilities for success, there's ways forward. I could see an open door and bound through it!"

He said, "yes, but what if it's the door to the psycho geriatric unit Annie?"

I said, "well there's worse things."

She was sat here. Same thing, like a photo, all the gear.

She said, "Oh, have you come back again to check on the Little Gems?"
I said, "no. I'm beyond lettuces..."

She said, "I've been thinking about what you said - about helping a poor struggling fellow being. I'd like to do that. I mean - why not...?"

I had his favourite souvenir t-shirt in my bag. I didn't put it there deliberately mind! I just tucked it in with the other things without thinking...

So I said, "here, you could return this to its rightful owner."

She said, "who is its rightful owner?"

I said, "a vicious and highly unstable psychopath."

She seemed a bit doubtful. I said, "don't worry, you've got certain attributes which might win his trust."

Anyway she hummed and ha'd - but she went.

She said, "I'll pop back and let you know how he takes it."

Been gone a while now.

Went off there... disappeared through the trees. Just like a trick of the light...

Christine Watkins. 1999.

LUCY GOUGH

Lucy Gough was born in London and spent her early years in Beddgelert before the family settled in Bath, where she attended a convent school. She left school at fifteen and a year later returned to Wales, this time to Fishguard. There she followed an Open University course in Drama and in 1982 moved to Aberystwyth where she graduated with a degree in drama in 1985. As part of her degree, she wrote a play called *Bad Habits Die Hard*, about a naughty nun, and started work on the play *Joanna* which she finished as part of the M.A. in Playwriting which she gained from Birmingham University.

She has written several stage plays which have been professionally performed, including *Catherine Wheel* (1991), *By a Thread* (1992), *As To Be Naked* (1994), *Rushes* (1995), *Stars* (1995) and *Wolfskin* (1997). In 1994 *Crossing the Bar* was shortlisted for both the John Whiting Award and the BBC Wales Writer of the Year Award.

She has been commissioned to write a number of radio plays, many of which have also been staged: *Our Lady of Shadows* BBC World Service (1997); *Prophetess of Exeter* BBC World Service (1998); *The Red Room* (with material from Glyn Hughes) BBC Radio 4 (1999); *Mermaids* (with material from Marina Warner) BBC Radio 4 (1999), *Judith Beheading Holofernes* (with material from Germaine Greer) BBC Radio 4 (2000).

For the last four years she has been scriptwriting for Mersey T.V.'s Teen soap *Hollyoaks* and lecturing in Radio Drama at the Department of Theatre, Film and Television, University of Wales, Aberystwyth. A volume of three of her plays has been published by Seren Books.

THE RED ROOM

The Red Room is based on a radio play of the same name, broadcast by BBC Radio 4, 1999. In the radio play, Charlotte Brontë's interior monologue was interwoven with biographical material on Charlotte Brontë (provided by Glyn Hughes) and on the cataract operation her father underwent at the time of her writing of *Jane Eyre*.

Charlotte Brontë	Rachel Atkins
Father	Eric Allen
Producers	Peter Leslie Wild
	and Rosie Boulton
Director	Peter Leslie Wild

THE TAIL

The Tail forms part of a radio play, *The Mermaid's Tail,* broadcast by BBC Radio 4, 1999. In the radio play, the mermaid's interior monologue was interwoven with documentary material by Marina Warner on the mythology of mermaids.

Girl	Alison Petit
Mother	Sunny Ormonde
Boy	Tom George
Producers	Peter Leslie Wild
	and Rosie Boulton
Director	Peter Leslie Wild

The Red Room

By Lucy Gough.

CHARACTER:

CHARLOTTE BRONTE.

SETTING:

The setting is the interior of a room that the Brontes have rented whilst Charlotte's father has an eye operation. It has a mirror, a large apostles cupboard, and a writing desk as well as the bed on which her father lies. During the monologue Charlotte goes to an imaginary landscape of ice and snow. This should be suggested by lighting changes and sound-effects.

Charlotte is the only one on the stage, although the setting should be such that the presence of her father in the bed, the surgeon and his nurse are suggested by what Charlotte is saying.

Scene 1 THE ROOM

Charlotte enters the room. She looks around unhappily, opens a window and looks out. After a while she shuts the window, turns to look at the room again, and sighs in despair.

CHARLOTTE:

I will suffocate here,

Melt into the floor.

Die of loneliness.

as she lights a candle

The shards of my heart,

Stuck fast in the wax of my dying.

she looks around and paces forward

There's barely room to pace, three strides and my path is blocked by furniture.

The bed stretches like some insurmountable peak, and the heads on the apostles cupboard flicker reproachfully in the candle light like disembodied ghosts, intent on haunting me.

she reaches the mirror and looks into it

Only the mirror suggests another world, a vast region of emptiness, of dark caverns and space to breath in.

longingly

To be standing on a moorland crag, breathing in the fresh air and feasting on the sweep and swell of a familiar land.

slight panic

How am I to find a place where my mind can wander?

she looks around in despair

This room has all the appeal of a tomb.

She starts to pace the room as if agitated and trapped like an animal in a cage

I walk the floor.

Stalking imagination as it treads corridors.

Hiding under its cloak,

as the graveyard of memory is visited.

Cling fast as it searches:

For that place.

That comfort.

'Angria'.

The country of my childhood.

Her pacing changes to crunching on snow. A cold wind is heard and the lighting changes.

shivering

I pace and pace.

Pace and pace.

Slowly...

the sound of trudging footsteps on the snow

Into the landscape of my imagination.
Charlotte blows out the candle. Blackout.

Scene 2 THE MIRROR

*Lights come up on a new day. Charlotte walks over to the bed
and sits beside it. The impression is that her father is in the bed,
and the surgeon is at work on his eye. She takes her father's
hand and looks into the mirror facing them.*

CHARLOTTE :

How still we look. How resigned, framed by the gilt of the
mirror, like figures in an oil painting.

she describes the figures she sees.

A frail old man, his hand held by a plain dutiful daughter. How
brutally each detail of the room is repeated, even my novel, my
hope for immortality lies unwrapped beside the water bowl. A
testament to my failure!

But how little of the story does the mirror tell. Nowhere does it
speak of the deep, dark despair that roams, aimlessly plucking
holes in my heart. Nor does the icewax of my father's face
plunge the depths of his terror as he faces the scalpel. Only the
red of the damask curtains speak of a brooding passion, and the
mountainous white pillows of a cold fear to overcome.
And the surgeon.

She studies him.

As he works, the mirror studies him, he has the look of Wellesley. He'd go into battle or make love with the same assurance.

she is cross with herself

Even the walls blush at my thoughts. How well the mirror holds my little crooked face, and hides its scorching passion.

If I were to sit here naked would he notice me? Would he touch my breasts as tenderly as he drops the belladonna into my father's eyes?

He studies his own reflection as he washes his hands.

with envy

To be so sure of one's face, to be able to study the features without fear of disappointment. He fills the mirror as he fills the room. The rest of us shadows in his background. If he was lying here instead of my father, if he was blinded. I would nurse him, my plainness concealed in the way my passion is now. He looks at my reflection, the plain Jane; if only he would look at me with something other than disinterest. Am I condemned to the transparency of a governess forever?

pause

The mirror holds its breath.

pause

He cuts as if through ice.

pause

How still my father...

pause

How steady the surgeon's hands.

pause

As the white of the eye turns red.

starts to breathe fast, panicking inside

The sun burns red

making the room swim blood.

The apostles heads dance with the dread of it all.

And my soul tries to leave the room.

trying to calm herself

Still.

I must keep still.

I must cool this fever of imagination.

she speaks slowly, trying to calm herself

If only I could pace,

Walk the room.

Still.

I must keep still.

Though every sinew cries flight!

close to having a panic attack

Still.

I must keep still.

As courage fails me...

on the edge of panic

I will have to get up,

Let go of his hand,

Leave the room.

Flee!

argues with herself

I can't!

firmly

I must stay here.

firmly

I must keep still.

she calms herself, breathing slowly

Tread slowly into my mind.

Crawl out to the edge,

Seek refuge

In the landscape of imagination.

Blackout

Scene 3 THE START.

The room is stifling. Just the tick of the clock is heard as Charlotte paces to and fro.

CHARLOTTE:

Time stretches across the room.

Fixing me in its sticky threads.

I count the movement of the clock.

I count the throb of my tooth.

I count each wheel judder as it passes the house,

And time spins patterns intricate in its boredom.

Her soft pacing build during this speech as the light changes to cold white. Again she goes to the ice landscape.

His courage shames my despair.

As wilfully I seek escape.

My restless mind darts around.

In this red hot stale stillness.

I tunnel the darkness.

Pacing becomes faster and more frantic.

Searching.

Searching for a place to run wild with my imaginings.

Her pacing becomes harder, with more effort.

I tread slowly,

Crawl out to the edge,

Seek refuge.

She is relieved as she reaches the ice

In the landscape of imagination.

She is walking on snow

Why does my mind persist in haunting this landscape?

Why when I search for the burning clime of Angria does this polar region spark my imagination?

What is it that pulls me to these fields of ice?

Has despair glazed my thoughts?

My spirit frozen with loss of hope!

Trudging in the snow

Why does the emptiness?

The bitter chill.

The savage bite.

The starkness.

The endeavour needed to walk it

Draw me here and

Feed my imagination?

Why have I conjured a landscape

So vast,

So lonely?

I feel orphaned by its immensity.

Which even in all its strangeness feels familiar.

Briefly she sits at the desk and writes

"Jane, Eyre."

She stops writing and goes back to the snow, looking around, puzzled

What story begins to write itself as I fumble my way through this terrible, beautiful place?

Have I the courage to step further into this territory?

Has the red heat of the room,

The lack of space,

The inactivity,

The fear,

Brought me to the very edge of imagination?

she walks on the snow

To a place so extreme, so uncluttered, so submerged I can start to form ideas of my own. "Shadowy like all the half comprehended notions that float dim through children's brains, but strangely impressive…"

I feel that all of passion and grief lie in this place.

But first I must find it,

Face it.

Then heave it back over the threshold!

Fade to blackout

Scene 4 THE ICE.

Charlotte is still traipsing across the snow, the cold wind whistling around her.

CHARLOTTE :
looks around anxiously

Which way?

No signposts, no paths to follow.

Just an endless reservoir of frost and snow!

shivers

I should have wrapped myself in fur.

Lost in this death-white realm, lightly dressed and no notion of where I should go.

Snow melts in my shoes.

The only heat the throb of my rotting tooth.

I shall be lost forever!

No landmarks to guide me back.

For what reason has my mind brought me here?

What story is this writing?

Maybe Angria lies buried under the snow. If I dig deep maybe I will find it.

she starts to dig in the snow

This snow is so deep.

as she digs

All I wish for is the comfort of that childhood country hidden from me.

blows on her cold hands

My hands are so cold.

she digs again

Deeper maybe it will be deeper.

Hard ice, this is hard ice.

she sees something in the ice where she is digging

Something...

I can see something...

A shape underneath.

The outline of a form, half covered.

shock of recognition

Maria!

My dear sweet sister frozen under the ice.

she scrapes the snow away

Her pale white face as clear as it was.

So little changed.

Cold white purity.

Her bloodless arm clearly visible,

I could almost touch it,

Rub warmth back into it.

See life spark in those blank eye-hollows.

But why does her shattering death inhabit this land?

A blizzard starts. The corpse of Maria is covered by snow again.

The snow returns her to the ice of memory.

How to reconcile this image?

The corpse of my sister frozen under the ice…

She starts to sketch out letters in the snow:
R…E…S…U…R…G…A…M

'Resurgam'.

I write a quiet hope for resurrection.

She writes a section of Jane Eyre

I still recoiled at the dread of seeing a corpse.

"Helen," I whispered softly, "Are you awake?"

She stirred herself, put back the curtain, and I saw her face, pale, wasted, but quite composed: she looked so little changed, that my fear was instantly dissipated. Her forehead was cold , and her cheeks both cold and thin, and so were her hand and wrist.

Silence. Blackout.

Scene 5 THE DUTY.

Charlotte pours water from a jug into a bowl, dip a cloth into it and starts to wash her father.

CHARLOTTE :

as she washes her father

How frail he looks, lying here,

Helpless,

Sightless.

A giant brought down.

And how much more tenderly do I love him. Seeing the frailty of the man.

wistful

If this was Heger[1] I was bathing, if he was rendered blind and needed my care my love.

she is ashamed of her thoughts

This room nurtures thoughts I'd rather not own.

In her anger at herself she scrubs roughly, then hears a noise outside. She goes over to look, pulls back the curtain to see but is taken aback by the brightness.

I'd forgotten how bright daylight was.

She describes what she sees to her father.

It's a wedding, a young man is lifting his bride out of the dust into a carriage.

horrified

Her veil has caught on the carriage, it is torn.

Blackout

Scene6 THE PASSION.

Charlotte is again walking on the snow. The blizzrd can still be heard..

CHARLOTTE :

A dark shape,

Perches on the horizon.

Its jagged edge taking shape in my mind.

As it becomes clear it fills the landscape,

changing it.

As she works out what the shape is

A man on a horse.

Has Wellesley[2] left my childish land to visit me here?

Or is it Heger that haunts my imagination?

Am I to write passion and rejection in equal measures?

On the ice landscpe there is the sudden sound of a horse's hooves as it charges headlong across the snow, as if it is going to ride over her.

CHARLOTTE :

Will he cause an avalanche? Will the weight of it overwhelm me, suffocate me in the snow of my own thoughts?

He rides this tundra with a passion I dream of.

The snow melts around me at the sight of it.

Look at how his riding cloak is silhouetted against the moon.

The way his collar frames his face.

How do I write him for this extraordinary journey?

The horse thunders past her

He rides past he doesn't see me...

annoyed

Is he blind?

firmly

In this story he sees me!

I shall wrestle this passion to the ground.

Transform him.

Write him with wings or,

wickedly horns!

I can do anything.

scornful

To condemn all wives to the fire: what sort of novel is that?

She catches a glimpse of her reflection in the mirror.

CHARLOTTE:

Who is that mad woman staring back at me from the mirror?
Unbridled passion swirling around her like a blizzard. Did she
escape from the polar region, did I unleash her with my visit
there? Is this expedition too dangerous? As I unlock memory do
I also unlock madness that should be shuttered away in those
recesses of the mind that none visit. Those recesses which we
batten down and keep watch over. I don't want madness to be

the price of love, and she will burn holes in the snow if I let her traipse it, but now I have conjured her she is part of the journey.

she is struggling across the snow, breathless with the effort of it.

I struggle across this land.

Laden down with images

of dead sisters, torn veils, felled giants, caged heroes.

Of fire and blindness.

But it's all too huge.

The light of the story, the tiny flame at its centre...

I cannot find....

The struggle gets harder.

I scale peaks.

Teeter precipices.

The cold of it all gnawing at my soul.

But the tiny flame at the centre if it all eludes me.

Though I want to
I cannot leave this icy place.

I heave onto this cold blank canvas, images of great passion and detail.

But they do not meld.

And this journey leads me to despair!

climbing

Why has this place confounded me?

Blackout

Scene 7 THE THAW.

At first Charlotte is sitting at the desk writing, and then she travels again out onto the ice.

CHARLOTTE :

she writes

My eyes where covered and closed; eddying darkness seemed to swim round me, and reflection came in as black and confused a flow.

Charlotte moves from the desk and is now hacking fiercely and desperately at the ice. (It may work better for this to be simply a metaphor for her writing)

as she hacks

I hack hard, but the iron ice will release nothing.

My hand aches with the cold and the effort

But all thought, like my heart, lie petrified in the frozen water.

From the ice,

I look back through the hard glass of the mirror,

Into the red room.

And I see my soul staring back.

Fractured from it's centre.

Together we see my heart burning inside the ice.

The cold will of duty freezing it, in its grip.

My soul tells me the heat is not passion but revenge

said with deep feeling and understanding

And I see the shards of the heart that Heger splintered.

she drags and heaves fuel onto the ice

I will carry onto this frozen wasteland all the pain and hurt that love has wrought me

I will fight back, not with tears but fire

I will win what is mine and in so doing shift the fracture, willing my soul to slide back to its place at the centre of my being.

she starts to build a fire

I build a fire on this cold place...

She lights the fire, and blows on it to make it burn. We hear it crackle. The ice begins to melt. Suddenly she falls through. She struggles in the cold water, sometimes gasping for breath from the cold. There is an exhilaration in her voice.

I plunge into the cold shock of understanding.

As the bones of the story lying scattered across the ice, start to take shape.

I sense the restless movement of my mind is the journey it will take.

I recognise that I must read the gravestones of memory to experience them again in the writing.

That I must wrestle with the pain and humiliation of love and rejection.

Write those deep dark moments!

I understand that this ice landscape is not the place of the story but the territory of its mind.

That this hostile clean landscape and the courage needed to cross it,

Like some arctic explorer

intent on great discovery.

Is the reason for its existence.

In this ice-cold water of understanding I can feel the true core of myself.

I can feel the pain, the raw bite of memory.

And I can see the path through duty and passion...

It is called 'HONESTY AND REVENGE'.

THE END.

Endnotes:

1 Constantin Heger: Professor at the Athenee Royal in Brussels. Charlotte Bronte fell in love with him during her stay in Brussels. The love was unrequited.

2 Arthur Wellesley: Son of the Duke of Wellington, and king of Angria in Charlotte Bronte's early stories.

The Tail

By Lucy Gough

CHARACTERS:

MERMAID (GIRL): A young girl on the edge of womanhood. She is slightly anorexic.

THE SHIPPING FORECAST: The announcement from the radio.

As a bath is filled the girl steps onto a scales to weigh herself.

GIRL:

Stupid scales.

reassuring herself

It'll be less with me clothes off.

She undresses, letting her clothes drop onto the floor, and steps onto the scales again.

in despair:
It should be less than that with all this off!

She steps off the scales and starts to tune her radio. The bath is still running and is nearly full. The radio plays in the background. The girl is cleaning her teeth and mixing the water in the bath as she sings 'Bobby Shaftoe' tunelessly. She tests the water in the bath. It is too hot.

Ouch!

She runs more cold water into it and then tests it again. She gets into the bath.
She goes under the wtaer for a minute, then back up to float in the bath.

I float.

Float,

Flesh,

Bone,

Hair,

I float.

Lighter than air.

Float in the bath.

Hair draped around me.

I float.

Like the Lady of Shallot.

She disturbs the water

Or a fish.
Silence as she floats in the bath. She studies her naked body in the mirror, moving in the water.

Skin stretched silver.

Ridged over bone.

I float.

A pale white corpse,

Mountain ranges breaking surface at their tips.

As an underbelly of coral leads to a dark triangle of submerged forest.

she moves in the water

Sometimes...

Suddenly revealed by the tide pull.

Folds and ridges fall either side,

As the sea erodes the edge.

Carving it.

Shaping it.

A long Atlantic ridge merges...

Skin turning bone...

silence

I could disappear,

Float away.

the girl sloshes some water out of the bath

Dissolve in the water,

Sink without trace,

Be swallowed up.

Who'd care?

she hold her breath under the wtaer and re-surfaces

A pale naked corpse...

Carving my shape...

she goes under the water determinedly holding her breath, then comes up again. She looks towards the door as if talking to someone on the other side of it.

You think you know who I am.

What I want to be.

What I want to do with my life.

But you're wrong.

completely wrong.

silence

I swallow words…

Skinning each one as it rises,

Gutting it.

Boning it.

Holding words down,

down deep in my belly.

Sustaining myself on a feast of silence.

On the flesh of unspoken words.

Having to be different.

If I try, if I try and hawk up the words, they lodge in my throat like shells.

Only silence can truly express the hugeness of this.

You don't understand me,

understand what it's like, all this changing.

Your words shoal like mackerel,

Darting through the water.

Changing...

Changing.

Silently.

Shapeshifting...

defiantly

I swim caverns.

The girl, now a mermaid, goes under the water again. She holds her breath, determined to stay under. In the water she struggles to breathe. The effort of swimming, and of willing herself to change shape and grow a tail, is apparent.

MERMAID:

I fast
flesh into fish.

As I turn.

underwater

Turn bonesack,

Turn skinscale,

Turn tailfleck.

Feet web,
As,

Under the water,

Flesh dissolves,

And scales barnacle into a seaskin of gossamer armour.

I turn

Into a shape that binds me,

wraps me.

A scaly smelly fish tail.

Concealing.

Entrance meshed,

Forests submerged,

Bony nakedness,

Turns,

In a heaving groundswell of change.
As layer binds layer.

Taunt skin turns scale,

With the swell of the sea,

Flesh turns bone turns fish.

A violent bloody change.

As slimy sticky scales fix to me.

And I scallop shapes from my skin,

Sweeping, swirling scales.

Carved out from my flesh.

Each one,

Marks me.

Claiming my body as my own.

In a ritual of change.

To choose a bony prison,

of scaled armour.

To deny the flesh,

and fast into fish.

To be safely chained,

with a tail.

To swim oceans of mind and deny this other world.

Is to disappear.

She is swimming with confidence and then finally comes up for air. The shipping forecast starts on the radio (with the pips). The mermaid turns the radio up. She sinks into the bath to listen to the shipping forecast. We hear her tail flipping in the bath water. She submerges herself; the shipping forecast becomes muffled and is then drowned out. During this scene the mermaid is gradually swimming further out to sea, which becomes stormier as the shipping forecast is read. By the end she is struggling to swim in a huge, stormy sea.

SHIPPING FORECAST
Atlantic high, South East Iceland. 3 to 4. Fair to Good. Lundy Fastnet, fair to good. German Bight north-west 4. Viking, variable sea area. South Utsira, North Utsira, fair to good.

MERMAID:
she swims with ease now, fairly close to the surface

Slimy liced scales of mother-of-pearl,

mirror the sea.

Rendering invisible my long thin body,

as it purls the water.

Its boned carcass, ridged,

Jutted,

Sharp.

Cuts its way through the seas,

On,

towards the Cromarty.

SHIPPING FORECAST.

Tyne, Dogger, fair to good 4 to 5.

MERMAID:

swimming

Dancing the Dogger.

Dogfish cutting their milk teeth on my tail.

Waves barking as they carry bones down,

Down to the sea bed.

Where I picnic with Angel fish,

nibbling on sardines.

Gnawing on bones.

Picking on flesh.

swimming

On towards the Cromarty.

SHIPPING FORECAST.

Portland, Plymouth. North westerly. Variable Sea area, Fisher, Viking, Strong winds 6 to 7.

MERMAID:

she is swimming; the sea is slightly rougher
Fisher wrestles Viking.

Ships burn.

As the fetch of each wave carries me on,

Over the fury of it.

On towards the Cromarty.

SHIPPING FORECAST.

Atlantic low west of Shannon, Mallon, Hebrides trough effect. Irish sea.

Fair Isle warm front, thirteen hundred...

MERMAID:

Past the fair Isle who brushes her hair.

Glimpsing reflection in the glassiness of her sea.

SHIPPING FORECAST.

North westerly, German Bight . Fair, storm later. Fastnet, Rockall, storm arriving.

MERMAID:

under-water, near the surface. storm slightly stronger

Under the sea,

Forests of fish, flee Fastnet's.

As the rugged Rockall harbours wrecks.

That chain stock the seabed.

SHIPPING FORECAST.

Thames, Dover, White. Atlantic high. Faeroes...

Forth Forties, Faeroes, Force 7 to 8, high winds, storm later.

MERMAID:

the sea becomes rougher. A large sailing ship passes by on the fast current, sails flapping in the wind

Eddying on the fast current to the Faeroes where a golden ship carries the dead,
gypsum masked,

stacked in the bows,

bound,

wrapped, ready.

SHIPPING FORECAST.

Sole to Shannon storm now, becoming good later.

MERMAID:

swimming into a bigger storm
Ready

For their Souls to sequence swim.

Freed from their husks.

And Gold leaf children,

Souls wrenched unripe from their shells

perch a fore deck.

sound of swimming

And on,

Onto the deep, dark sea of the Cromarty.

she swims, struggling against the storm

I swim them all.

Towards the Cromarty.

SHIPPING FORECAST.
Biscay. Bailey. South East Iceland.

Fastnet, North westerly force six.

MERMAID:

beginning to sound stormier; crashing waves. She is struggling
And on.

SHIPPING FORECAST.

Moving slow over Rockall.
To Lundy, and Malin head.

<u>MERMAID:</u>

And on.

she plunges deeper under water; the storm is raging
And on to the deep dark place of the Cromarty.

SHIPPING FORECAST.

Irish Sea gale warning 7 to 8. Hebrides, Malin, storm force
nine...

MERMAID:

The Cromarty.

Where shipwrecks lie dying.

And devil fish pluck fins from others.

SHIPPING FORECAST.
Storm warning for Malin, Rockall. Cromarty. Severe force ten.

MERMAID:
*the storm is full-on, crashing waves, wind etc. she struggles with
the water*

And dark memories lie locked.

she dives down to the bottom

On the sea bed.
*the mermaid goes deeper. The storm sounds begin to be lost as
she dives.*

Silently,

I swim,

caverns blacker than pitch.

swimming down towards a ship wreck

I swim down,

down into the shipwreck.

Through windows shuttered by seaweed,

And doors open to the sea.

To an abandoned memory,

anchored to the sea bed.

swimming through the wreck

I can't see anything, there's nothing in here.

she touches something and screams

There's something horrible here.

she feels it

Papery dry.

Whose tail?

But it's dry like a husk,

Its scales turn to dust in my hand.

horrified

Mermaids don't die.

sifting through

All this silt,

bits of gold comb,

hair,

Shards of mirror.

realisation

I wanted to be a mermaid because I didn't want to change.

I didn't want to grow up.

But I didn't want to die

firmly

I know I don't want to die.

she struggles to swim up to the surface. She is gulping for air and wrestling with the heaviness of the water as she tries to surface. Her tail is being shed as she heads upwards.

GIRL:

struggling

Up and up,

I must swim upwards.

struggling

Surface,

Get air.

As my tail unravels,

each scale like a chain-link falls away

making me lighter.

The freedom wrench draws blood.

But as the tail sheds so does my fear of it all,

Falling heavily like an anchor into the seabed.

The dark murky water of the deep is clearer

I can see light above the surface.

The sinew and muscle of my legs thrust me upwards,

As I taste the saltiness of life,

Its blood, sweat and tears.

The girl breaks through the surface. She gets out of the bath, dries herself a bit, then opens the bathroom door and shouts to her mother:

Stick the kettle on Mum.

THE END.

One Woman, One Voice

LUCINDA COXON

Lucinda Coxon was born and educated in Derby. Her first play, *Waiting at the Water's Edge,* re-connected her with her Welsh heritage and with the experiences of her Welsh-speaking grandmother who had, as a young girl, left her home in Rhydyfelin to go into service in England. The impetus for *Waiting at the Water's Edge,* premièred at the Bush Theatre in 1993, was the dramatist's reflection on her grandmother's dispossession of language and country. *Waiting at the Water's Edge* was performed by Made in Wales Stage Company at The Point, Cardiff, in 1995. It has been published by Seren.

Her next play for the Bush Theatre, *Wishbones,* published by Methuen, was *The Sunday Times*'s 'Pick of the Week' throughout its run in 1997. Other works include a stage adaptation of Tarjei Vesaas's *The Ice Palace* (1994) for the Royal National Theatre, published by Methuen, and *Three Graces* (1995), premièred at the Lakeside Theatre, Colchester. She has been writer-in-residence at the University of Essex and is currently working on *Fascinating Gism*, a new play for South Coast Repertory Theatre, Southern California. Her feature films include *Spaghetti Slow* and *Lily and the Secret Planting*. Her screen adaptations for British Screen include *The Dyke and the Dybbuk, The Echoing Grove* and *Mother of Pearl*.

I AM ANGELA BRAZIL

I Am Angel Brazil was first performed at a Royal Court Workshop, 1998.

Angela Brazil	Karl Johnson
Director	Simon Usher

It was subsequently performed at the ASK Theatre Projects, Los Angeles, 1998.

Angela Brazil	Michael Winters
Director	Veronica Brady

I am Angela Brazil
by Angela Brazil

I AM ANGELA BRAZIL BY ANGELA BRAZIL is a piece for a woman in her mid-forties, to be played by a male actor. The performance should be in no way camp. The actor should have access to a glass of water but drink only as specified in the text.

––––––––––––––––––

A tall chair, like a comfortable bar stool, and a glass of water in the centre of an otherwise bare stage.

A general lighting state up on the actor playing **Angela**. *The actor stands away from centre stage, speaks directly to the audience.*

ACTOR
Hi... hi - I'd just like to say that I am not, of course, Angela Brazil. But I will be her for a time, tonight, to the best of my abilities.

We felt it best that I portrayed her, so that you might engage more fully in her story without the embarrassment - the inhibiting self-consciousness, the thing that makes you want to look away, that brings <u>you</u> shame when <u>she</u> started it - that sometimes rises up when listening to the intimate, perhaps nonsensical, or just plain unprovoked, un-called for details of a stranger's life.

So tonight, you do not need to look away. Because the shame is all Angela's, and she is not here. And she is, in any case, well able to bear it.

And if you wonder why, at any point, why I am sitting in that chair, being Angela, and telling you all the things that I will be telling you...

well that's simple.

It's because that's how Angela wants it.

Thank you.

The actor sits on the stool. A new lighting state. Angela takes a moment to focus. Then:

ANGELA:

I am sitting in the house - not house, no - bungalow - where do these words come from? India, like kedgeree, bungalow - anyway the bungalow belonging to my husband's mother. It's a nice enough 'bungalow' - more absurd, each time, that... will we get past it? Well, we'll have to - double-glazed, no draughts.

My husband's mother's tastes are not what you might call sybaritic, no. For the most part she lives frugally. She is of her generation. She has a cupboard under the sink containing washed out yoghourt pots. Her life reads like a ration book.

And I am sitting in her home, and looking at a photo in an album. It is a picture of the bungalow, but taken from the outside, at about this time of year I'd say, the roses over but the fuchsia clinging on.

My husband is changing the lightbulb in the garage. His mother has a list of jobs for when we visit. Some of them need doing. Some she simply needs to know that she can make him do. Her husband is dead.

I don't blame her for these deceptions. If I were a widow with a son, I'd do the same. Or a daughter, come to that. It's human. I forgive it. In fact, I warm to her because of it.

And looking at the photo of the outside of the place in which

I'm sitting, I'm struck by a kind of déjà vu, displacement. I don't know why this triggers it, but I recall a dream I had this summer which has bothered me although I'm not sure why.

And the dream, it goes like this:

I am in my lover's house. I have slept there, thinking that it's empty, knowing him to be away. I was drunk and - very drunk, in fact - and needed somewhere to stay. I have broken in - or have the keys, perhaps?

In life this is not true - I don't have keys. I wouldn't want them. I couldn't help but use them for wrong reasons. In fact this dream might be the result in life of my actually having keys.

So perhaps that's what the dream's about. How good it is that I'm shut out. Forbidden. And I am forbidden. So perhaps the dream is to explain to myself why it's better this way, why I must be shut out for my own protection.

This house, is, of course, only one of many places to which I do not possess a key.

And a key would always be a penis wouldn't it? I mean if you were talking to some oaf who'd once leafed through the Fontana Book of Freud, they'd say 'the key is a penis, and you don't have one, so this is a penis envy dream'.

"You are, Angela", they would say, "whether you like it or not, a bitter woman".

No one wants to be bitter, do they? It's one of the things that no one wants to be. It's hardly possible to say it without screwing up your mouth. Without thinking of something dark and wrinkled that tastes of underarm deodorant. So I would rather not be that. And I don't think the key is necessarily a penis. In fact, I don't think there really was a key in this dream.

No. I prefer to think I've broken in. Because I would rather break and enter than be bitter.

And those seem to be my only options.

Angela pauses.

ANGELA: I'm sorry... for a moment then, my eyes were stinging. How embarrassing for you. How interesting for me.

So, I have broken, I have entered. Hah! Just like a man! Breaking, and entering. Forcing yourself on the unwilling house, despoiling, spoiling, soiling, soiled. Contaminating presence. Spoils the home. Wrecks it? Home-wrecking? Subconscious desire to... But no, this isn't me either.

It is hard these days to be ourselves.

Anyway: I wake up in my lover's house. And I feel bad - ill - yes - poisonous with drink - and self-disgust is rising in my windpipe - sour, yes. A sour thing in my throat, the thing that's left to throw up when you've thrown up everything else. The thing you can't get out. Then panic. God! I work out where I am. Should not be here. They'll be back soon. Him and his family, the wife, the kids, the whole shebang. And I'll be caught.

Catastrophe.

I go downstairs. Astonishing. I see I've made a mess the night before. I've been trying to cook something. The kitchen is - calamitous.

I remember vaguely. Acid flashes. Ugly scenes I have to bite down hard against.

And then I see it on the table, this extraordinary thing, and remember that I brought it:

a fish. I've brought a fish, a long thin silver one. It's big, at least three feet, and reminds me of one I saw dead on the side of the canal that runs through the industrial park where the bakeries are gathered so it always smells like morning there.

I walk by this canal with my husband sometimes, laughing at boys with fishing rods who wait for something to emerge from the treacly deep of the stagnant water, wait hours in freezing wind for some sad mutant thing to get hooked on their line. Nine times out of ten the mutants get away. I don't know why the ones that do get caught get caught. Are they sickly? Or is it just bad luck?

Or maybe as they get pulled closer to the surface they start to see the light and can't help wondering what it would be like to break that oily skin and rise into the white world, just as I stand on the bank and wonder about the dark.

And once the hook is in, a moment's curiosity can be enough to catch you off guard, with your drawers down, and then it's all just so much flapping and panting and looking in amazement with your unblinking eye as the truth of things comes into focus only then to slip away, taking a tantalisingly long time to vanish so that what at first seemed like climactic revelation turns instead to a sadistic torment.

"Come and have a look", they say, "at what you would've won". I don't watch TV if I can help it. I find it hard to follow.

So. This fish. Why did I take it there? Where did I get it in the first place? I can't remember in the dream, and looking back, I'm none the wiser.

I have no idea at all.

What does it mean to bring a fish here?

Well obviously, you're having a field day aren't you?

I've brought this raw and smelly fish flesh, slapped it on this family's kitchen table. You're not daft. You've made the link. You know how to follow the crumbs through the forest. It can only mean one thing.

To someone looking in from outside.

Inside this dream, things aren't so simple. Inside this dream things are allowed their weight. This dream does not read Sunday papers. This dream has never had a cappuccino. This dream is in no hurry to get home. This dream does not divide experience into two categories: threat or promise. This dream does not expect an experience for its money. This dream is neither your reward, nor mine.

This dream is better than you.

This dream is.

Look at me.

Who do you think I am?

Do we have anything in common?

Angela takes a sip of water and collects herself.

ANGELA:

So I come downstairs, and there, in the kitchen which looks, as my mother would say if she could remember what she used to say - 'like a bomb's hit it' - 'this room looks like a bomb's hit it'... there is this silver fish.

So did I bring it as an offering? Is it a gift? I go to a bookshop, I look in a dictionary of symbols. I memorise what it says. I could buy the book, but I like to memorise things, like to know I still can, and besides, with an investigation of this nature, you need to travel light.

"Fish." It says. "The fish has for long been regarded as a symbol of abundance and - by the Japanese - pluck".

Pluck.

We don't say 'pluck' any more. I realise that now. I'm struck how I always thought the old meaning of 'spunk' had gone out because it was replaced by a new meaning. But that's not it. We just don't need it any more.

Spunk, pluck. Wattle, daub.

When did that happen? What do we have now? 'Guts' I suppose. We have guts. 'I was gutted'. Back to my fish. My fish was not gutted. My fish was intact, perfect, but outside of the element it requires to live.

So have I brought this family a symbol of abundance?
 Had I forgotten they were away? Was I planning to feed them - and lavishly? But then why would I want to prepare a feast for the family of this man I am fucking, have been fucking now for some time, but may not fuck for a great deal longer -

Ah. Is that it?

I should have told you sooner, I've not been sleeping. It began in the summer: I would wake each night at four - or rather four o seven, on the dot. I was amazed at this routine. Four o seven without fail. Where is the clock kept? Is it the mind that wakes the body or the body wakes the mind? I wondered what would happen with the end of British Summer Time. Simple. Three o seven. And with the same thing in my head of course: the loss of something. A thing you never really had except for long enough to make you want it, already fading, almost out of sight.

Sometimes I wake crying for it and my husband comforts me. I can imagine how that makes you shift and shuffle. Well, judge not.

It's not the loss of love I mourn. Love's not like that. It's not like - dignity, for example, which can be lost like an umbrella or a glove. A moment's inattention, at a party, on a bus, and - pfut - it's gone.

Love's something else and easy to confuse with other things.

Like excitement.

Or like boredom, come to that.

So, have I seen the writing on the wall? 'Mene mene tekel upharsin' - the end of the affair? And do I come now with my fish to cook, to make amends, to serve and to translate myself into something safe? Before such a translation is imposed on me in any case?

Angela considers.

ANGELA

I could become a trusty - that's what they call them, isn't it? The criminals no longer thought to pose a threat. (A eunuch - if I were a man, but we won't start that again). That way there would be loss - yes. Yes. But not exclusion into the bargain.

I'd get away without salt for the wound.

But salt is antiseptic.

Angela falters, seems unsure of herself for a moment, but resumes.

ANGELA

Let's read on in my memory: "In Egypt the fish represented Hathor, the cow-headed goddess, who was supposed to control the rising of the River Nile, necessary to irrigate the crops. It also signified the principle of creation, and thus was a charm for domestic felicity".

Do I bring this family domestic felicity? I can't see that. I don't think I've ever brought anyone that. Spunk, pluck, domestic felicity. No.

But do I bring them fertility, or what remains of mine? Is this a Trojan fish, packed - packed - with roe! My lover's wife no longer able - though she's shown herself to be prodigiously so in the past - to conceive a child. And I, not much her junior, ten years, I suppose, with - what? - a year or two of good eggs left in me. Do I slap down this fish as a warning to her of the kind of havoc I could wreak and pass off as an accident?

Or is that accident my secret wish?

A fish is a good symbol for a secret wish.

Why isn't that in the dictionary?

I once read a story where a woman bit into a Fortune Cookie. Do you know what the message inside it said? "Your most secret desire is about to come true". Imagine that. Take a moment. What was it like for that woman?

Angela's eyes range over the audience.

ANGELA

Do you have many secret desires?

Which is the MOST secret?

Is it hidden even from you?

Is that a good thing?

Are there words to express it?

Can you know it without having a language to articulate it?

What keeps you from achieving it?

What would you sacrifice to fulfil it?

Does everything have a price?

Can you afford your secret desires?

Do they grow weak and leggy in the dark?

What would happen if they were out in the open?

Would you still desire them?

Would people laugh at you?

Are you a joke?

Angela lets this question hover in the air a while.

ANGELA

Your most secret desire is about to come true.

Is that a threat or a promise?

Which of these possibilities shall I rule out?

Is the river rising? Or draining away?

When I told my friend Margaret I was afraid of turning forty, she said, 'think what your mother was doing at that age. That always helps to put things in perspective'. So I did.

Angela takes a drink of water.

ANGELA

At forty years of age my mum was still two years off meeting dad. Three from conceiving me. She'd hardly begun the body of her life. So you see why, even now, with a flash of white hairs behind one ear, the roses over, but the fuchsia clinging on, I can toy with the idea of procreation.

But I only toy. Do not, if I am honest, look forward to the beginning of anything. I'd like to find out why that is.

Sometimes, now, I've noticed, I turn my back on him. This lover. Lover. That word too sounds odd. I ignore him, hoping to attract. Like a dog that wants to be chased.

It's an odd thing, to be finished with, as I am.

I remember at the start when we were trying to get the sex right,

I'd turn away from him in bed and moments later he'd be hard. But I'd turn back and things would fall apart.

Eventually we sorted all that out. I thought. But now, I turn my back again.

That's what animals do, isn't it. Offer their behinds as a gesture of submission.

Am I beaten?

My husband fucks me mostly up the arse these days. The lover I don't allow. Although it would be easier. He's smaller for a start. But I deny him. Not just because I can, though that's, of course, a part of it.

But it isn't only that.

I'm afraid of what it does to me, the paralysing thing, the fusing all the spine into a peg to hang you from. It makes me dumb, unable to talk even to myself. It jams my mind.

The relief is indescribable.

So that's where I find rest these days. The only thing that hits the spot. And husband's happy too, I think. I do not give him power so often he can afford to look sideways at such opportunities.

Ouch.

You're not warming to me are you?

You might, in time. I might tell you things to make you feel sorry for me. I could do that. Tell you things to make you put your hands up to your mouths, sit forward, lean in to me.

Listen.

When I'm quiet, when I'm just the sound of the blood in my ears, not looking at anything but the back of my own eyeballs, when I'm in that precious state... when when when when when father papered the parlour, when Santa got stuck up the chimney, when I fall in love when when... then - I am not thinking of the waste.

What is lost in translation.

Waste not want not. Wash another yoghurt pot.

Scald another jam jar?

Tear those knickers into dusters?

Fuck you.

Angela looks away from the audience. She is silent. Eventually she rearranges herself in the chair and:

ANGELA

So, I look around the debris of the kitchen. How can I have made this mess? How have I managed to bring myself to such disgrace? To such humiliation?

Everything I do to clean up makes things worse.

I can't see straight, I'm tired, my eyes won't focus. I scrub and brush and wipe but only seem to spill and scatter, vision fading in and out, a tide of tears like Vaseline that blurs and smears, eyelids like bad wipers on a wet night, driving too fast on an unlit road. The kind of drive, that when it's over, you can't sleep, you're scanning your blindness all the time for the tail lights of another car, for the paper bag that could have been a rabbit, for the bend in the road that should have been signed, for the skid that you've got to steer into if you want to survive.

And if I could get this place clean, restore it to a perfect state, then would that be enough? Or would they get back, sniff the air, and even though <u>nothing</u> was missing, even though <u>nothing</u> was out of place, immediately sense that I had been here?

Have I made it too clean? The lie betrayed by its sheer credibility. Its excess of detail. Watertight. No clumsy human element, no room to breathe.

"You try too hard", my mother used to say. "You give yourself away".

And what if they call the police? My fingerprints. They're everywhere...

This would be one of those cases left open and unsolved for years. It would become the particular obsession of a detective approaching retirement, with an otherwise unblemished clear-up rate. I'd be a marked woman. Any stupid misdemeanour down the line - drunk in charge of a Fiat Panda, exposing myself in a public place, stealing something I didn't even want from a supermarket, pressing the pillow over mother's face - and he'd be tipped off by some Brother at the Lodge, feed my pawprint to a computer and reunite it with its match.

Aaaaah... he's giddy with it - "Bring her in", he'd say. We'd meet. At last.

And he'd despise me.

All those years of fascination, and I would be so... ordinary. A riddle but no Sphinx. An anti-climax. And he'd ask "Why did you do it? How could you...?"

And I would say nothing.

He'd go home once he'd read me my rights and sit on his hand till the feeling had gone out of it, then wank himself silly and pretend the hand was mine.

Then he'd turn on the TV, the last disappointment in place, and let things take their course.

Everything I do to clean up makes things worse.

Why did you do it?

How could you...?

My mother's tissue paper frail. She pushes the skin on her forearms up like sleeves. How could you? I look at the other visitors sometimes, wonder: which of us has the stomach for it?

The nurse says its worse for us than the patients. They can't remember how much they've forgotten. I don't believe this. I think it's a lie and not a white one.

I worry about what happens when the visitors are gone, in the hum of low-level emergency lighting. I worry whether nurses are still 'kindness itself, they couldn't be kinder' when we're not there. Would I be? Would you? Be as kind? If people weren't watching? People whose sensibilities had to be spared. Who didn't have the stomach for it.

I used to think of arriving unannounced, surprising them, trying to catch them out. But what would I discover if I did? What would happen next? No point. In any case it'd be just the night staff sitting reading magazines, the women's ones, I've seen them on their desk sometimes.

About 'how to change your life'.

And 'how women live in other countries'.

'How to be better at sex'. A whole page of how to put a condom on a man without using your hands. Practice on a banana: start off with a green one, progress to the more advanced technique required for the sickly-smelling black-spotted overripe variety.

And how to recognise the early symptoms of rare but potentially fatal illnesses.

I changed my life. And it returned the favour.

I sing to my mother when I see her. Songs that come from places

I don't remember having been.

Angela belts out with gusto:

ANGELA

"When father papered the parlour,
You couldn't see pa for paste.
Slapping it here, slapping it there,
Paste and paper everywhere.
Mother was stuck to the ceiling.
The children were stuck to the floor.
You've never seen a blooming family
So stuck up before!"

Boom boom!

I sing that one a lot. Not just when I'm with her, but driving home too, in the car. I sing it LOUD! Loud as I can with the doors all locked and the windows shut. Loud as I can, in competition with the engine, and no one outside can hear a thing.

Isn't technology marvellous?

No, really.

The place we live in, it's a nice place but you hear the

neighbours snoring through the walls. Their cutlery scrape on their plates. The theme tunes of their favourite programmes.

When Father Papered the Parlour, When Santa Got Stuck up the Chimney, When I Fall in Love, When Johnny Comes Marching Home Again, When the Midnight Choo-choo Leaves for Alabam.

I count with my mother too. Numbers. One. Two. Three. Four. Five.

She cries when I reach a number she recognises: seven - oh! - seven! Or twelve. Twenty six. Fifty three. Ninety one.

Nothing over a hundred. Treble figures move her not at all.

Twenty six is a good one. I can't say why. I wonder what she was doing at twenty six, but I don't know and she can't tell. Dad's dead. There's no one left to ask. I cling to twenty six, but that's me stepping on a shadow. It slips away, no loyalty to twenty five or seven, let alone to anything beyond.

I don't know if she cries for joy, or if it's hurt: I've poked her in a tender place she'd forgotten she even had. But I keep poking.

Why do I? How can I?

Sometimes she sleeps while I'm there. I used to take this badly. But when she's awake she doesn't know me. When I leave she doesn't know I've gone. Why should her sleeping make any odds? I try not to watch. Her eyes move under their lids and it makes me wonder:

What do you dream of when you've forgotten who you are?

I don't talk to the other visitors, and they don't talk to me. It's not a club. You don't want to get too pally with someone whose thing in common with you is going to fracture their hip and succumb to pneumonia some time in the next six months. And there's a strong hereditary tendency with this illness. We're all tainted.

We don't draw strength from each other.

We keep to our old people. What we have to look back on. What we have to look forward to.

Why did you do it? How could you?

A long silence. Angela covers her eyes. She's upset.

ANGELA

I'm sorry.

I'm sorry... I...

She makes to get off the stool, but changes her mind... where would she go? She sits back but tries to shield herself from the audience.

ANGELA

I'm sorry, could you actually not...

Christ, if you had a puddle of humanity between you, you wouldn't watch this...

She's angry now.

ANGELA

Well, can you all see?

She looks up, genuinely distressed.

ANGELA

Are there people at the back who can't see?

She dips her hand in her water glass makes tear trails on her face. Sobs.

ANGELA

Is that better?

She stops sobbing, wipes her face dry.

There's something about me you don't find convincing, isn't there? I can tell some of you are sitting there thinking: there's something about that woman that's just not quite convincing. Not as if there's something she's not telling us - God, no, the opposite of that. As though she's telling us everything so we can't make head or tail of it. Can't see the wood for the trees.

Here is the forest! Where are the crumbs?

I'll tell you about the forest. When I was a child there was a shortcut home from school and my mother told me NEVER, EVER to take it. Not even if I was with the other girls. She meant it, I could tell. This was not a rule for no reason, and when she spoke to me about it, I felt inside myself an appropriate level of inarticulable fear.

But when I was with the other girls, the fear became exciting. We often took the shortcut. Once a month, at least. Although we'd all been warned, been told the same.

And whilst we set out on the path that cut across the forest laughing, we were quiet once we got to the dark place in the middle, and we ran the last stretch to the road.

And when I got home on those days, I would feel a glow of pride and shame all mixed up and I would watch to see if my mother could smell it on me. She smelled something - I tried too hard, you can imagine - used to give myself away, but she never knew for sure. And we could never have it out because my dad would find out then, and nothing must ever be done to upset him.

He was old - older even than her, and had flown a plane in the war.

His nerves were shot to ribbons. As they say.

He couldn't stand the sound of a bouncing ball, of a skipping rope tick on the concrete path, of raised voices, weeping, laughter, a whistling kettle or any kind of surprise. So my mother and I negotiated our secrets with a minimum of fuss.

Which is why I was amazed to arrive back one day - a day when I'd taken the long - the approved - way home - to find my mother waiting in the front garden, and to have her cry and throw her arms around me.

A little girl my age had been murdered in the woods. My mother had just heard. And while she hugged me, which was unusual in itself, my father watched from inside.

And that night in bed, I cried for the other little girl, who wasn't me but could have been, and although I didn't know her I believed that somehow, through my disobedience, I had played some part in her death. I had as good as killed her.

That fits in somewhere.

That's a part of it.

How I decided, so many years later, to put myself in the way of pain again.

Angela takes a moment, struggles to refocus.

ANGELA

So I'm sitting in my husband's mother's bungalow and I'm looking at a picture of the outside of the place in which I'm sitting, and she's pointing something out to me, and it's something I already know because she repeats herself all the time and she does it because she's lonely and I feel sorry for her, I really do, but my mind just slips its leash and then I'm back - back in this kitchen, in this eggs and flour and marmalade, and is that piss...? and I can't see, and the best I can hope for is to get out before anyone gets back here and I just CANNOT, CANNOT CLEAN THIS UP. And EVERYTHING I DO TO CLEAN UP MAKES THINGS WORSE. So I go to leave, but my fucking legs won't work, they won't fucking cunting bastard move, it's like gravity's gone up a gear, I can hardly even lift my chest to breathe... and then... and then... there's something stirring upstairs... the house isn't empty at all... a sigh, and legs stretch under cool sheets that I know are ironed by this "incredibly reliable woman from Bosnia."... the one who "needs the money she hardly speaks English what else would she do if she didn't come here she's grateful - a fiver an hour - paid in cash, it's not bad..."... but that part's not my problem, I say, that part I understand... no, my question is this: what kind of person can't make their own bed? What kind of person can't rinse their own spit from a basin? What kind of person can't wash their own cup? "Oh yes!", he says, "Yes! Turn this into a gender thing"... the breathing gets harder. "I have to consider what my time is worth!". .. Christ... "And it's different with kids." Wow! "And what would the woman from Bosnia do without people like us to make a mess to let her clean up to give her the money to live, and we're not talking join the glossy magazine-buying fraternity here, we're talking food in her mouth, we're talking shoes on her feet, we're talking, we're talking..." but we're not talking at all, of course, and I can feel myself turning my back. I push back my hips, because without the Rosetta Stone of sex I can't understand a word that he is saying.

Who does he think I am?

Do we have anything in common?

A stirring on the floor above, the house isn't empty at all, and then a rustling on the stairs, and people - so many sleepwalking figures - begin to appear.

I must - now - be discovered.

I brace myself: a young girl walks into the kitchen, smudgy still with sleep. His daughter, whom I recognise from a picture on his desk at work, but she actually seems to know me, she doesn't seem surprised to find me there. She says "I need to go to the toilet" and I become maternal in an automatic sort of way, trying to blend in with my surroundings.

I say "go on then, and I'll make you some toast." She goes out, quite convinced, to the bathroom.

I feel bad about this. I don't want to make friends with her. I don't want to make her like me. It's deceitful. I don't want her involved. I've tried, in fact, not to look at her picture, not to know what she looks like... I wanted to protect her from that. I don't want her to have to wonder who her father really is, like I did, perhaps... but I can't dwell on that -

now a young man appears - and there are others on the stairs who look just like him - not identical, but more or less the same. These are lodgers, in their dressing gowns. An enormous number of them. And I'm suddenly struck by the understanding that they are allowed here - all of them, and I, who had somehow thought myself close to the heart of things, do not belong.

These lodgers are so un-jealous of what they have, they don't even notice my intrusion. They wear their privilege lightly, don't feel the need to dress for breakfast. I had imagined they would chase me out. But they don't need to. They are simply indifferent.

This turns out to be, for me, the final straw. I am dizzy and confused, the kitchen spins, my eyes snag for a moment on the fish, oddly brilliant now, before I fall into a swoon - and wake.

My bed, at home. The neighbour snoring through the wall. I feel... hungover, nightmarish, disgusted. And afraid. But gradually these feelings fade, and what I'm left with is something different.

How I feel about things at the time and what they mean as I reflect are two completely different things.

We look up from the picture of the bungalow when something flickers from the garage, a big fluorescent tube that makes a sun patch on the dark drive.

"He's mended it", the widow says, her face lit up, her faith restored. My husband comes in, wiping his hands on a towel. I smile, struck for a moment by the thought of what a good father he would be. But I can't pursue this because in the back of my mind I'm wondering how it could have been light when I first looked at the picture of the bungalow and now it is really quite dark.

Don't we always imagine our dreams to last as long as they would in the waking life? To be played in real time? When the truth is they're over in seconds.

His mother returns with a can of own-brand lager she bought specially.

She turns on a lamp. Cosy.

He's checked the oil and water in her car, topped up the anti-freeze. Filled up a bucket with coal, taken the heavy box of ashes out of the grate.

She apologises for not wearing the cardigan we bought her last Christmas but it needs cleaning and she hasn't got round to "taking it in for an estimate".

We let this go, although neither of us understands. Does she not like the cardigan? Can she not afford the dry-cleaning? Is it a project she's built up, a thing to not get round to so that she can feel busy? Or has she so lost her confidence, become so unworldly, unsocial without company that she wouldn't know how to go about this simple task?

She's seen a programme on the TV - "you know it the one with the fat girl" - about women who can't stop crying. Any tiny sort of thing can set them off, she says, the good as well as bad. They can't read papers, watch the news, can hardly go out in the street in case they witness some miserable scene. And they're ashamed of their crying but that only makes them cry the more.

She says she could become like that herself. She thinks we all could.

I think of the little boy at the bus stop in the dirty school uniform with the smacking great bruise on his face. "I thought we would be friends again..." But his mother pushes him away, she's drunk, she stinks, bare legs, high heels, huge saggy tits no bra, and everyone at the bus stop watching. And the tears on the little boy's face and I smile at him and she says: "Is that lady being nice to you? Do you want to go and live with her? She wouldn't want you long once she found out what you were really like".

"No - I'm sorry", says the child, "I'm sorry. I thought we would be friends again..."

The widow's off down a new road now: "That pop singer that killed himself in Australia... That girlfriend, his wife... She's had a lot of personal tragedy in her life."

Why does she care about this?

How does she even know about it?

Didn't people like her used to pass their old age knitting squares for the Brownies to stitch into blankets for people whose homes had been scuppered by earthquakes? Being useful?

Why does she care about all of this CRAP?

I'm consumed by the urge to start up When Father Papered the Parlour. But I don't.

And the next thing I know, my husband and I, as they say, are back on the road, with everyone else. Making our escape, heading for the city on a Sunday night. Glad to be hurrying somewhere where you can't see the stars, and where no one in your street knows what school you went to, what your parents look like, or how you came to be sick on your espadrilles at a party in 1972.

I'm driving. My husband's asleep. He's relaxed when I drive. He believes I'm a good driver. He trusts me. He's right to do that. Whatever you might think.

I like motorway driving on cold nights. The car heater blowing on the steaming up windscreen, the wipers' rhythm, the tyres' hiss. A sense of something in common with other drivers, all of us travelling in the same direction. And I think what it said in the Dream Compendium that I looked at in the cut-price bookshop where the shoe repair man used to be: "If several fish are seen swimming, many people are working to help you".

It talks about seeing a single fish too...

But there's a flash of brake lights up ahead and I have to slow suddenly, stretch this arm out automatically across my husband's chest, to stop him lurching forward, waking up. I protect him from that.

I am courteous to other road users. I dip my lights, I don't hog lanes, I flash people and let them in, I mirror, signal, I manoeuvre, yes, but more than that, I smile. Through the window. Wave an appropriate acknowledgement for kindness shown, like this -

She does so.

Through the rain-spattered rear-view.

On nights like this I'm glad my mother's given drugs to make her sleep. I'm glad the broken bird of her's sedated in the bed, not up and out and flapping in the storm.

I love my husband very... no, I'm not going to say that to you, it sounds too... it isn't what I mean... it doesn't do justice, do credit... My husband and I, that's our own concern.

He is a good, warm, honest man.

I shouldn't have to tell you that. You shouldn't, in fairness, expect it.

But there are frozen places in me. And I tried hard to thaw them but in the end you need someone who'll swing an axe. Who won't mind hurting you. I found a man like that. Who'd give me something to cry about.

And the axe blow nearly finished me.

I didn't know your heart could get this hot. I should have guessed. When you think how hot the mouth, the cunt, the inside's unexpected temperature then, God, what steaming stuff inside the ribs.

We get home and I park the car. The house is as we left it.

I put the left-overs the widow gave us in the fridge. "I'll never eat that. I only get it in for you." In a couple of days, I'll transfer it to the bin.

Into bed. The neighbour snoring. Sleep, sleep. My husband lets me warm my cold feet on him. Sleep.

———————

To see a single fish is a lucky dream. It denotes "increased prosperity, a devoted spouse, and a brilliant child".

Angela shrugs.

ANGELA

When I think of the dream now, all I recall is the fish. The ugliness is only there as a thing to be redeemed.

By the perfect fish.

Which is also the fish from the canal bank, with its side all pecked out by the pigeons. Regenerated somehow through the magic of the mind.

Made fine.

I endure.

And at three o seven, when I wake and want to snap open my chest bone and let out the thing that's thrashing here, inside me, I do not.

I bite down, I contain it, I trot out the mantra.

And just because I sought this pain out, that doesn't mean it doesn't hurt.

But so far, I survive it, by putting myself in the way of more.

I lie still - three o seven. Three o eight. Three o nine. Three ten. Three eleven. Three twelve. Thirteen. Fourteen. Fifteen. Sixteen. Seventeen. Eighteen. Nineteen. Twenty. Twenty-one. Twenty-two. Twenty-three. Twenty-four. Twenty-five...

I say over and over: more love, more love, and I steer myself blindly into the skid - more love, more love - and I open myself up as wide as I can to it, and eventually the thrashing hits some kind of topnote, and dies.

Angela takes in the audience. She gathers her strength.

ANGELA

So I am Angela Brazil, and I was here near the end of the twentieth century, when we wept for people we didn't know and sometimes despaired of those we did.

And I broke and entered into your lives, stole in, disguised - forgive me, it's a very human subterfuge, in the hope that you would feel something for me. Learn something, even, perhaps.

Because I wanted to tell you: that something slippery and indefinable was once revealed to me.

It swam out of the darkness and defied all explanation.

And I don't know now if it means everything, or nothing. But I sit down before it like a child, and let it light me up.

And I hope that someday, somehow, each of you... whoever you are... may have the same.

Goodnight.

Angela Brazil lowers her head for a moment, takes counsel with herself, climbs down from the tall chair.

The actor acknowledges the audience in whatever manner seems appropriate, and leaves the stage.

One Woman, One Voice

GWENNO DAFYDD

Gwenno Dafydd was born in Bangor, Gwynedd, grew up in Pembrokeshire, and was educated at Fishguard Comprehensive School, the Polytechnic of Wales, Pontypridd, and the University of Wales, Cardiff, where she gained an MSc in Social Sciences for her study of the barriers encountered by five female stand-up comics in their working lives. She has also studied voice, improvisation and movement with Cicely Berry, Mary Hammond, Sonja Keller and Ida Kelarova. She has worked

Gwenno Dafydd, No Regrets

extensively for television, both as an actress and a presenter, and has also contributed widely to both Radio Cymru and Radio Wales. In the field of Theatre in Education, she has directed, acted and devised projects for Welsh learners in the primary schools of Dyfed, Gwent and South Glamorgan. Amongst the companies she has performed with are The Natural Theatre Bath, The Whodunnit Theatre, Triangle Theatre and Magdalena. She has also worked with groups and bands such as Bol D'Avoine, Peledr X, Rendezvous and Cabarlatsio. A talented singer, she has performed at numerous festivals, events and international cabarets, and has been commissioned by radio and television companies to write lyrics for specific projects. Her fluency in French, along with her acting and singing experience, led to her being offered the lead role in a play about Edith Piaf at the Sherman Theatre, Cardiff, in 1987. Eluned Phillips, a long-time friend of Edith Piaf, saw the show and has since been very supportive of Gwenno's writing and acting career. The fantastic media reception to the play also inspired Hedd ap Emlyn to persuade Gwenno to perform in North Wales, and rather than just performing the songs, Gwenno decided to create a narrative with which to link them together. The result was *No Regrets*.

Her stage work includes *You Can All Love Me* by Caroline Gawn, which she performed at the Sherman Theatre in 1987, and *No Regrets*, performed at the Studio, Theatr Clwyd, in 1988.

NO REGRETS

No Regrets was premièred at the Studio, Theatr Clwyd, 17 April 1988.

Edith Piaf	Gwenno Dafydd
Director	Gwenno Dafydd

Gwenno Dafydd translated the work into Welsh and performed it extensively during the summer of 1988, entitling it 'Llwyd Bach y Baw'.

No Regrets

by Gwenno Dafydd

All lights switched off. Total darkness.

(Piaf, in a childlike voice)

"Mama, Mama. Where are you? I'm afraid, don't leave me here. I'm so scared. I can't see you, I can't see anything. Mama, you won't leave me all alone will you ? Mama, I'm so afraid."

I was blind for three years, confined to a dark lonely cell, locked in the shadows of my mind. Yet, in the dead of that night, I learnt to feel things in all their intensity; words, sounds, sensations, all taking on a new distinct meaning. Now, when I really want to savour a song, I close my eyes and my other senses take over. I'm convinced that my journey into darkness gave me a different perspective from that of most people. I know things they don't know.

But what do you know of me? Sensational stories read in the press. You see what you want to see and hear what you want to hear. Only I know the difference between fact and fiction. I was born Edith Giovanna Gassion, daughter of 'The Great Gassion', acrobat extraordinaire, extraordinaire in his prowess for fathering bastards, nineteen in total, and made an entrance into this world on a policeman's cloak at midnight on a street in Paris. I was destined for the street from that point on.

Sits down. Legs akimbo. Slug of wine from bottle.

My mother didn't hang around for long after that. She was too busy whoring in the gutters and Papa returned to the filthy boredom of the trenches. I was left with her mother Aicha, she used to have a trained flea act with a travelling circus. That's where I got a taste for booze. She'd give me some wine diluted with water in my bottle every morning. When Papa found out, he dispatched me off to Normandy to stay with his mother. She was a cook for her cousin - who kept a whorehouse.

That's where I lost my sight - I saw nothing - heard everything. The whores loved me, thought I brought them good luck, treated me like a mascot, made little rag dolls for me. I got to know each doll separately with my fingers. The tarts took me to the ocean, waves thrashing and sucking on the shore, grains of sand trickling through my fingers like water I could hold on to.

I regained my sight three years later,
 She crosses herself.

Thanks be to God and St Therese.

hearty laugh

... Lisieux had never seen such a sight - all the tarts, walking one behind each other dressed in their Sunday best, to pray for the sight of a scrawny wretch. You know, when St. Therese grants a prayer you can smell the scent of roses ... no smell was ever sweeter, and the first thing I saw was the white black white black white keys of a piano ... a sign perhaps of what was to come ?

Then my father claimed me and dragged me from dance halls to bistros, alleys to squares. I was his partner. He taught me the tricks of his trade and I'd sing a bit and pull in the crowds.

Jumps up and performs as if trying to draw in a crowd on the street

"Ladies and gentlemen, you're in for a real treat now. Come and see the Great Gassion, the artist himself is going to work before your very eyes, You will never have seen such skill, such daring, such bravery. Now, who will donate a hundred centimes, so that we can begin..."

still standing

It's a hard life, but what an apprenticeship. I learnt how to feel an audience, how to draw them close to me and keep their attention. If we earned enough money after eating we'd sleep in a cheap pension, otherwise we would have the stars as an eiderdown. You learn how to survive, how to steal scraps of food from barrows and sleep rough in damp and draughty cellars.

Yes, you're free on the streets, no one pushes you around. My half sister, Simone, or Mamone as I called her, same father, worked in a factory for eighty four francs a week. Eighty four franks, why I could make that much in an evening...

naughty wink

singing.

"Tell you what kid, come and join me. I'll give you 15 francs a day and your board and lodging. I ain't doin' no more gymnastics and I've taught myself to play the banjo, after a fashion, I've fallen out with Papa - he says I'll never make an acrobat - says all my talent's in me throat and none in me limbs - so, I'll need someone to go around with the beret, now what do you think?"

We made a good team, even when I was 15, I sounded like a crow first thing in the morning.

shouts very hoarsely to Mamone

"Come on Mamone, you know I'm no good till I've had my Gargyl and coffee. It shouldn't take you long to get that ten francs we need, even with your voice. We haven't got a sou left from last night - wine doesn't grow on trees, more's the shame."

Running away from the cops, staying up till the first metro, falling asleep on dustbins, singing in the barracks, every sunrise a clean page waiting for the adventures of the day. We were cold, we were hungry, but we were free. Times were good in those early days on the streets. We had dreams to keep us warm and wine to keep the spirits up in those back streets of Paris.

1)   *Sous le Ciel De Paris*

Cradling baby in her arms

"Mama loves you, Marcel. There, there don't cry little one. Mama's here, Mama's here. Sh, sh, sh, I won't leave you my beautiful little baby. I'll stay close to you. Sh,sh,sh, sh, Marcel. Mama's here. Mama's here."

Quiet

"Mamone, she's not breathing... I'm scared... her heart's gone quiet... her brow's gone cold... Mamone, my baby's dead."

Scream of anguish

Imploring the audience:

Ten francs is all I need - won't any one of you give me ten franks. Please, please, help me. I can't give you anything in return - I won't squander it this time, I promise, I promise.

Bringing a small bunch of flowers to the grave

"Marcel, my baby, these are for you. How can I live now that you're gone? Blue eyes - your blue eyes smiled at me - they say if they get through nine days they'll be all right. You smiled at me, the eight days nearing nine and I thought the nightmare was over - but it's only just begun.

It jerked, your head, from side to side as I sawed with a nail file. I had nothing left of you so I sawed and sawed and saved a lock of hair - still sweet and milky smelling. Cold empty blue eyes - just another number in a morgue.

Ten francs, I needed ten francs more to bury you. My friends did what they could but they were all as poor as I was...a stranger's coin on a bedside table ... love had never cost me so much… but what price a mother's love?

Marcel, my little girl. I wasn't much more than that myself when you were born, Louis and I were just kids, sixteen year olds playing at being parents. No one showed me how to be a mother, I didn't know how. I gave you so little and you gave me more than I've ever had before. Everything I've ever needed. A part of me died with you.

You gave me your unconditional love, never questioning, never doubting, never judging. Forgive me. I really did love you… to hold you close, your skin so velvet soft, your dancing smile and clowning antics … who would have thought such trivial things would be so irreplaceable, so priceless."

The bottle and I had always been companions, but after I buried my baby Marcel was the first time I ever got blind drunk. Four neat Pernod's knocked on their heads and soon the straightjacket of pain binding me loosened itself. I now knew the way to forget … In time, darkness turned to light and whenever the shadows overcame me, I could escape … and forget … if only for a while.

2)   *La Goualante du Pauvre Jean*

"Mamone, you'll never believe what's happened. This toff comes up to me in the street, said he heard us last night and he

wants me to sing in his night-club... his bleedin night-club!
Wrote the name down on a scrap of newspaper and gave me a
ten franc note... you heard of a place called Gerny's...?"

Talking with her reflection in a hand mirror

I can hardly believe it, look at you now Edith Gassion. No, I'm
not Edith Gassion any more, I am

with a grand gesture

'la mome Piaf'. You know, it doesn't sound so bad. I think 'Piaf'
has style. It'll look great in the headlines... 'Piaf sings from the
top of the Eiffel Tower'... ' Piaf takes America by storm'

a rip roaring laugh

 you can dream - they don't cost a penny, girl. To think all this
might not have happened if Leplee hadn't stopped to listen to
me singing on the street. He's been so good to me, just like a
father. I know, I'll call him Papa Leplee.

jumps up and looks around excitedly

He's made all of this possible. Oh, I'm so excited, a fine dressing
room, my own pianist, a real audience that's come to listen to
me... just me. No more standing on street corners, catching

colds, running away from the gendarmes. Yes, we've made it, Mamone. It'll be fur coats and fancy crocodile shoes for us... my name up in lights, just you wait.

The men will come flocking like moths to a flame... I can have any man I want now, legionaries, soldiers, sailors, there's plenty to choose from and you do, oh you do, Jaques, Louis, Albert, Yves, Claude - different names but not so different in the sack, an uniform draped across a chair back.

to someone in the audience

"Come and have a drink with me and my sister, soldier. Come and play leap frog on the Avenue Carnot. We'll stop off in every café from one end of the street to another. We'll dance, live for today and drink away your miseries. Forget the raids, the black market, the identity cards marked with a swastika. We'll give you some memories soldier!"

3) L'Accordioniste

Hands behind her back as if they have been padlocked before she was pushed into a room. She rubs her sore wrists.

When the bastards pushed me into Papa Leplee's room, I didn't know what to expect. He looked so elegant, his silver white hair immaculate - you'd never have known he was dead if it weren't for the congealed mass of blood where his eye should have been. I nearly choked on my tears. Even in death, with a bullet lodged behind his temple, he looked so handsome and well groomed ... he could have been asleep.

she rushes forward as if going towards the body

"It can't be true, Papa Leplee, it can't be true."

the interrogation

"I didn't do it, I didn't have anything to do with it. Why don't you believe me? ...George the Algerian? Yes, he was my lover... I introduced him to Papa... he killed him? No, I never told George anything about the safe... I'd never have done anything to harm Papa. Nothing, without him I'd be nothing. I loved him so much and now he's gone."

Times were hard then. Newsreels captured the interrogation. Nowhere to hide. The press hounds smelt blood and I was the kill.

she shouts like a street hawker

"Was the little sparrow the murderess ? Night club singer implicated in Leplee murder"..."Read all about it, read all about it!"

But I wouldn't let them destroy me. I had tasted the sweetness of success and the rancid decaying stench of the gutter was no comparison. Times were hard... No one wanted to book me... singing in intervals in cinemas... dead end provincial towns, peripheral in their potential.

But things got better, Raymond Asso came into my life and arranged my date with destiny. He had seen the tarnished star potential and set about transforming me, I fell in love with him... such sensational blue eyes... he beat me up... but then that's what love is like, surely ? Three years is all it took him to get me top billing at the ABC and once that happened, success was guaranteed.

There were times of celebration, concerts, tours, champagne gushing like rivers in winter, celebrities queuing up to shake my hand... Marlene Dietrich... she gave me a little green cross encrusted with emeralds... blessed by the Pope... who'd have thought eh, Mamone ?

she shouts like a street hawker

"Piaf takes America by storm" - read all about it, read all about it.

And finally true love came in my direction. I had waited so long. There had been so many men but so little love, men who wanted me because of who I was and what I could do for them. But this one was different. Very much his own man, he refused to try and impress me. He didn't need to *(laugh),* he even wore the jumpers I knitted for him. He wore purple ties and spotted shirts and taught me everything that matters about life. He was married with children, but it was me he loved, me. I'd never been so happy, life finally seemed worth living, and I was intoxicated with love. How could a boxer, such a brute of a man, be so gentle at the same time?

kneeling down to pray to St. Therese

"St. Therese, I ask nothing for myself as nothing could surpass the love that now surrounds me. I will enter a bargain with you. Leave me the suffering and pain and in their place give him his victory, you know about all his sacrifices, give him the victory he so rightly deserves."

Roses, a strong smell of roses surrounding me days later, and I knew that all would be well.

as if presenting him to the world

Marcel Cerdan, World Champion Boxer.

4)   *Mon Manege a Moi*

I had more happiness in those two years than in all the previous thirty...such a generous man, not just with his money but with his time and love... he taught me how to love myself, as well as others. We went to Coney Island.. he took me to the scenic railway... the crowd recognised us.

Various American voices shouting out

"Ain't that that guy, the boxer? The new world champion ? Gee it sure is. It's Marcel Cerdan. Hey and that must be Edith Piaf with him. Sing us a song Miss Piaf. Would you sing 'La Vie en Rose', that's my favourite? Yes, sing 'La Vie en Rose', my gal loves that one!"

5) *La Vie en Rose*

She tries to steady herself by a small circular table

"Dead... he can't be... No, no it's not true, he's not dead. He loved me. he wouldn't leave me like this... Oh, if only I hadn't insisted he come on that plane, he'd still be alive now. Mamone, I killed him, it's my fault..."

moves to table, sits down and puts hands on a glass on the table

"Marcel, are you there? Give me some sign so that I know that you're there... I sang for you the night you died... at the Versailles... did you hear me... I felt you were there... when I collapsed you picked me up didn't you? Speak to me. Let me know that you can hear me. I still love you Marcel. Please speak to me."

"Mamone, I'm sure the glass moved... I could feel the vibrations... I didn't imagine it did I... why should the table trick me? They never come in the daylight, but they do come at night don't they? I'm sure I felt him brush past me... felt his presence. I'm sure he was here, but why didn't he speak to me, why didn't he speak?"

the glass moves

"F...e...b...r...u...a...r...y... It's a sign Mamone, it's from Marcel... its February, and some numbers a one... a seven... then another one, then a nine, a five and finally a zero. It's the same as last time, the same date keeps appearing. Something will happen on February the 17th 1950."

A doorbell rings. Piaf moves away from the table, picks up a telegram and reads it.

"My dear Edith. Meeting essential. Come to Casablanca. Sincerely yours, Marinette Cerdan, dated February 17th 1950."

fade to black

Piaf addresses the audience

So I took the first plane I could and met Marcel's widow. We fell into each other's arms and cried whole rivers of tears. Did you think she was going to hate me? Well you never knew Marcel - Marinette and I shared a bond, a bond so strong that not even death could weaken it. Have you ever loved someone so deeply, so desperately that you needed just to share the same space with someone else who felt the same? Memories repeated over and over to make them come alive. But no matter how hard we tried to draw him nearer, his spirit remained elusive.

return to table

I can't go on without you. I've never felt so lonely in all my life, the pain is suffocating me, I can't bear it - I want to die. Marcel, listen, I have a song just for you.

She sings song to him through the table, with hands spread out facing each other, eyes looking towards heaven.

6)Hymne a l'Amour

That's when it all started going downhill. Cerdan's death nearly destroyed me...

Careless and reckless, I carried on living ... trying to forget, ... trying to join him? Horrendous car crashes, "How did she get out of there alive?" broken bits of humanity... pain ... torment ...agony... led to ecstasy and relief with the drugs, ... Morphine, an easy Master to please... I resigned myself to servitude

...Cracked mirrors... digging in my brain...hammering in my skull ... creeping on all fours... foaming at the mouth... find my fix... *(screams)*... find my fix

As if injecting herself with a syringe

Instant hit *(gasp)*... Instant ecstasy... no more pain... forget... remember...hit *(gasp)*... ecstasy... no pain... forget... remember... And before I know it, I'm on the carousel to hell.

She lights a candle to St. Therese on the table

"Saint Therese, release me, I pray, from the chains which enslave me. Haven't I kept my part of the bargain for Cerdan's success? I'm just a child, don't make me suffer any more. I know I have lived my life in a state of public sin, the men, drink and drugs, but I beg you to find it in your heart to forgive me and give me the courage to conquer the drugs which are destroying me."

7) Padam Padam

Piaf in a childlike voice echoing the beginning of the play

"Mama, Mama. Where are you? I'm afraid, don't leave me here. I'm so scared. I can see you, I can see everything. Mama, you won't leave me all alone will you? Mama, I'm so afraid."

That's how I killed the demons. My mother, who abandoned me when I was a baby, finally appeared to me when I needed her most. I saw her pock-marked face and ravaged body screaming out for her fix and knew that she had died alone... her body dumped on the pavement for the local morgue to pick up.

Talking to Mamone on the phone from the States

"Mamone, it's Edith... New York... How are you? ... Good, good... Yes, the tour went well... Carnegie Hall was wonderful. I had a standing ovation for seven minutes, Mamone... seven minutes... It seemed like forever... felt like waves of love... I gave them everything... right down to my very core...

Jaques? Well, things haven't got any better...yes I still love him, but you know me Mamone, I can't love any one more passionately after four years than I can after four days... it's difficult to keep a marriage alive when we're both away touring all the time... so, I've decided to ask him for a divorce... yes I'm really sure... He could never replace Marcel, I was foolish to think that he could... I have to go... speak to you soon."

Piaf is lying in a bed, recovering form one of her numerous operations, she talks as if responding to a surgeon's questions, she has five red balloons tied to the bed

"A little tired but in good spirits...

She nods to the balloons

Doug brought them for me... he carried them all the way through the subway... my Papa always promised me red balloons... but I never had any... *(long pause)*

Was the operation a success?...Complications? What do you mean?... further tests? Biopsy?"

Piaf on the phone with Mamone, from her bed

"Mamone... I don't know how to tell you this... Bad news...The doctors have found cancer...Yes it's true. There's nothing to be done, it's gone too far to cure... I'll finish the tour... Don't try and stop me singing now, it's all I've got left. I'm leaving hospital this afternoon and tonight I'll record Milord, just as I'd planned."

quite weak at this point, but nevertheless gives an outstandingly gutsy performance

   8)*Milord*

Dances slowly around with the doll given to her by Theo Sarapo

"I don't deserve this sort of happiness. You gave me this doll Theo Sarapo. Why do you love me Theo? Why do you want me to be your wife? I don't deserve you, I wasn't looking for you but you found me.

You're like a lighthouse, guiding me away from the rocks. So this is what real love feels like? I've waited so long. I don't care about the gossip, let them talk. "She's old enough to be his mother." What do I care... I'm old before my time, my body worn out through constant abuse. I can offer you nothing but pain and sorrow... you deserve better... a young girl your own age... why do you love me?

All these years I've longed for love. I really loved Cerdan, but if I was to be honest to myself, he would have left me and gone back to his wife if he hadn't died. They all leave eventually... You won't leave me will you my love? I couldn't bear the darkness without your smile. You brought me dolls, posies and you combed my hair. Your hands so gentle when they close my eyes."

9)   *Autumn Leaves*

Talking to Mamone on the phone

"Hello Mamone, it's Edith... Not well. I'm growing weaker all the time, Mamone, come and see me... Couldn't you come before? Isn't there anything you could do to come earlier?... Tonight, you'll come tonight. Good.

Oh, Mamone, I really want you to meet Theo, my earthly saint, my husband Theo. It's my wedding anniversary today Mamone. This year has been the best year of my life. I've waited so long to find love and it's nearly too late. I've never been happier in my life and I've never been so sad. I can see my life trickling away like grains of sand through my fingers... I want to live so much for Theo, God, how I want to live, Mamone, there's not much time left, I can feel it... So you'll come tonight?... Good."

Puts phone down

"St Therese, I pray, leave me a little longer with my love."

   10) Mon Dieu

Piaf is on her death bed, her hands clawing at a blanket

"Mamone, oh I'm so glad you came... Having you here is so good for me ... little sister. We started off with nothing, ha, look at me now, at one time highest paid female singer in the world. ...All that money and where's it all gone ? Drink, drugs, men, hangers on, they all took their share and left me with nothing but memories.

Do you remember; Claude frying eggs for my breakfast on the Arc de Triomphe flame?... meeting Charlie Chaplin... my songs made him cry... my blue satin bedroom... the fashion houses where we bought two of everything... Guerny's... that tablecloth wasn't meant to be a shawl... hiding my fix in the gramophone pick up... the strawberries in kirsch and melon in port... coin on the table... singing from the top of the Eiffel Tower ... who would have thought eh?

...so many memories, Mamone...was that really my life ? but I have paid the price of pleasure and my price was pain...it was my desire to live that devoured every ounce of life in me...

feasting like a cancer...old age won't capture me...I spit in its eye...my flame will have burnt out long before it can claim me...my voice recounts my experiences...the anguish of my soul...pain my currency...my life a long journey in search of love...all leaving their mark...but so few of them giving me what I really looked for, love.

Love conquers all Mamone, and life's too short for regrets."

    11) Non, Je Ne Regrette Rien

Spotlight full on for song, then at end Piaf collapses and the lights go out

Gwenno Dafydd 10th July 2000

Lost For Words by Sarah Snazell

Sarah Snazell was born in 1965 and was brought up in Abergavenny by her mother. As a child she loved to walk in the Black Mountains, which later formed a backdrop to much of her work. In 1984 she went to Newport to do an Art Foundation Diploma, and the following year moved to Leeds to study Fine Art and History. She completed her MA in 1995, exhibiting in Yorkshire and Wales. Although she regularly travelled back to Wales frequently, regarding Abergavenny as her spiritual home, she settled in Leeds with her partner Hugh. She taught art in local colleges as well as becoming a local arts organiser and painted at Jacksons Yard studios in Leeds. In 1996 she won Cymru Ifanc for the first time and was invited to become a member of the Royal Cambrian Academy. In 1998 she was diagnosed with Breast Cancer. She died the following year.

A longer appreciation of the work of Sarah Snazell can be found in Planet 139, 'Sarah Through the Looking Glass: The Art of Sarah Snazell' by Anne Price-Owen.